Aristotle on Life, Aging, and Mortality

Aristotle's Insights into Memory, Sleep, and the Mysteries of the Human Mind

A Modern Translation

Adapted for the Contemporary Reader

Table of Contents

Preface - Message to the Reader

Rebuilding the Greatest Library in Human History

Thousands of years ago, the Library of Alexandria was the heart of global knowledge — a sanctuary where the wisdom of every known civilization was gathered and shared freely.

And then, it was lost.

Now, we're rebuilding it — and you are invited to join us.

At the Library of Alexandria, we've set out to make every book available to *every person on Earth* — not just in print, but in every language, every format, and for every reader.

Here's how we do it:

- **Deluxe Print Editions at True Printing Cost** - Order any book as a high-quality paperback, elegant hardcover, or stunning boxset — and only pay what it costs to print. No markups. No middlemen.
- **Unlimited Access to the Greatest Works** - Enjoy thousands of timeless classics — from Plato to Shakespeare to Tolstoy — in beautiful, modern eBook and audiobook editions. Read and listen without limits — for every reader, everywhere.
- **Modern Translations for Every Language & Dialect** - We're reimagining the classics in clear, accessible language — and translating them into every dialect imaginable. Everyone deserves to understand humanity's greatest ideas.

When you visit **LibraryofAlexandria.com**, you're not just accessing books — you're joining a global movement to restore, preserve, and share the wisdom of civilization.

Join us today at LibraryofAlexandria.com

Together, we'll ensure the light of human wisdom never fades again.

With gratitude,
The Modern Library of Alexandria Team

Visit:

www.libraryofalexandria.com

Or scan the code below:

On Youth and Old Age

Aristotle's Reflections on Aging and Human Development

A Modern Translation

Adapted for the Contemporary Reader

Aristotle

Translated by Tim Zengerink

Introduction

Ancient Greece was a civilization famous for its great contributions to philosophy, politics, art, and science. It thrived from the 8th century BCE until the Roman Empire started to decline. Greece's city-states, especially Athens, were the heart of culture and intellectual thought. This was the time when democracy began, impressive buildings like the Parthenon were built, and famous playwrights like Sophocles and Euripides produced their works. The Greeks' curiosity about the world around them laid the foundation for Western philosophy. Thinkers like Socrates, Plato, and later Aristotle, pushed the limits of what people understood about the world.

Greek society was deeply connected to theism, which focused on a large group of gods and goddesses who were believed to control every part of life. But this system did not prevent people from exploring new ideas. In fact, it coexisted with a growing interest in finding logical explanations for nature and human

life. Intellectuals would often debate and discuss these ideas in public places like the Agora. Aristotle grew up in this dynamic environment, learning from earlier philosophers, and later challenging and expanding their ideas.

Aristotle's Life

Aristotle was born in 384 BCE in a small town called Stagira, located in northern Greece. His father, Nicomachus, was a doctor for King Amyntas of Macedon, and this allowed Aristotle to be around the Macedonian royal court from a young age. When his parents passed away, Aristotle was sent to Athens at the age of 17 to pursue his education. Athens was the center of intellectual life in Greece, and Aristotle joined Plato's Academy, which was the most respected school of the time. The Academy was a place where students discussed everything from ethics to science. Although Aristotle learned a lot from Plato, he did not always agree with him, especially when it came to metaphysics, which deals with the nature of reality.

After spending almost 20 years at the Academy, Aristotle left Athens around 347 BCE after Plato's death. He traveled around different cities in Greece, continuing to study and learn. In 343 BCE, he was

invited to the court of King Philip II of Macedon, where he became the tutor of Philip's son, Alexander, who would later become known as Alexander the Great. Aristotle taught Alexander about philosophy, ethics, politics, and science. Aristotle's influence is visible in Alexander's leadership style, which showed respect for knowledge and strategic thinking.

After teaching Alexander, Aristotle returned to Athens in 335 BCE, where he opened his own school called the Lyceum. Unlike Plato's Academy, the Lyceum focused more on recording knowledge and observing nature. Aristotle and his students performed research, studied animals, and took notes on what they observed. The Lyceum became a major center of learning, and it rivaled Plato's Academy. This is also where Aristotle wrote many of his famous works.

Later in life, after the death of Alexander in 323 BCE, the political climate in Athens became difficult for Aristotle because of his connections to the Macedonian court. Accused of disrespecting the gods, Aristotle decided to leave Athens. He fled to Chalcis, where he passed away in 322 BCE. Even though he had to leave Athens, his legacy lived on through his many writings and the influence of his school, the Lyceum.

Aristotle's Impact on Western Thought

No figure looms larger over the development of Western philosophy and science than Aristotle. A student of Plato and tutor to Alexander the Great, he unified logic, ethics, politics, rhetoric, and metaphysics into a coherent system that shaped intellectual inquiry for centuries. Although his writings reflect the best knowledge of his era, they also reveal a distinctive way of understanding the world—one that balances observation with rigorous logical analysis. Over time, this method has profoundly influenced everything from political theory to modern scientific methodology.

Aristotle approached knowledge as an interconnected whole, seeing each field of study as a vital path toward truth. While many earlier thinkers focused on abstract concepts, he emphasized direct observation of the natural world. By systematically examining and classifying what he saw, Aristotle laid the groundwork for the empirical methods now central to modern science. Although our understanding of nature has evolved, his legacy endures in today's emphasis on evidence-based research.

Logic: The Foundation of Rational Inquiry

Often hailed as the "father of formal logic," Aristotle introduced a system of reasoning that shaped intellectual discourse for over two millennia. In works like the Organon, he analyzed how valid conclusions are drawn from premises and introduced syllogisms—deductive arguments that became standard tools in philosophy, theology, and science. Even contemporary logic, despite its modern mathematical and symbolic advancements, can trace many of its core principles back to Aristotle's pioneering analyses.

Metaphysics: Exploring the Nature of Reality

Aristotle's Metaphysics offered one of the earliest comprehensive explorations of existence at its most fundamental level. There, he described the nature of "being qua being" and introduced the concepts of potentiality and actuality to explain how things change and develop. These ideas deeply influenced medieval scholastics—both Christian and Islamic—who integrated Aristotelian reasoning into their theological frameworks. Today, discussions about consciousness, identity, and free will still reference these Aristotelian notions.

Ethics and the Pursuit of the Good Life

In the Nicomachean Ethics, Aristotle proposed that the ultimate aim of human life is eudaimonia, often translated as "happiness" or "flourishing." He argued that we achieve this through virtue, developed by cultivating good habits guided by reason. His famous Doctrine of the Mean asserts that moral virtue resides between two extremes—for instance, courage lies between recklessness and cowardice. This focus on character formation has profoundly shaped the tradition known as "virtue ethics," influencing modern debates on moral education, personal development, and what it means to live well.

Politics: The Role of the Individual in the City-State

Aristotle's practical approach to ethics naturally extended into political theory. In Politics, he explored various forms of government—monarchy, aristocracy, oligarchy, democracy—and weighed their merits and pitfalls. For Aristotle, a well-ordered polis (city-state) exists not merely for survival or trade but to enable its citizens to live virtuous, fulfilling lives. His conviction that ethics

and politics are intertwined remains influential, informing contemporary discussions on citizenship, governance, and justice.

Rhetoric: The Art of Persuasion

In his treatise Rhetoric, Aristotle examined how persuasion works, detailing how arguments must appeal to ethos (credibility), pathos (emotion), and logos (logic). This clear framework for effective communication continues to guide public speakers, legal advocates, and writers. From ancient courtroom orations to modern political campaigns, Aristotelian rhetoric underpins many of the strategies people use to sway audiences and shape public opinion.

Beyond these core subjects, Aristotle made significant contributions to biology, physics, psychology, and aesthetics. In the Poetics, for example, he investigated why humans respond so powerfully to tragic drama, pioneering the concept of catharsis—the emotional release that audiences feel through art. Throughout the medieval period, thinkers like Thomas Aquinas integrated Aristotle's theories into Christian theology, while Islamic philosophers such as Avicenna and Averroes preserved, interpreted, and expanded upon his works.

Across centuries of reinterpretation and debate, Aristotle remains a living voice in contemporary thought. His insistence on systematically gathering evidence and connecting it to logical principles laid the foundation for what we now recognize as the scientific method. His inquiries into human flourishing, civic responsibility, and the nature of argument continue to spark discussion and inspire new research. From personal ethics to societal organization, Aristotle's ideas help us frame enduring questions about how best to live, learn, and understand reality.

In sum, Aristotle stands as a foundational pillar of Western thought. He bridged abstract theorizing and practical inquiry, bequeathing a vision of knowledge that values both reason and experience. From ethics and politics to science and art, his ideas have been woven into countless intellectual traditions. Even today, as we grapple with questions of morality, governance, and truth, we walk in the footsteps of an ancient thinker whose breadth of insight and depth of analysis continue to guide our pursuit of wisdom.

Final Thoughts

By preserving Aristotle's legacy, we protect the intellectual depth and rigor that defined his way

of understanding the world. His systematic way of asking questions, his classification of knowledge, and his ethical theories are still relevant today, providing a model for critical thinking across many subjects. This preservation is important not just for philosophy students but for anyone interested in the foundations of human thought and the development of ideas that shape the world we live in.

One of the difficulties in studying Aristotle's work is that his ideas and language are complex. Translating these works into our modern language is a key step in making his profound insights easier for more people to understand. By putting his ideas into today's language, more readers can engage with his thoughts, even if they don't have a background in classical studies. Making Aristotle's work accessible means adapting them to modern ways of thinking without losing their original depth. This helps bridge the gap between ancient and modern readers, making sure Aristotle's work stays relevant.

Section 1

We now need to talk about youth, old age, life, and death. We will probably also need to explain the causes of breathing, since living and dying sometimes depend on it.

We have already explained the soul in detail elsewhere, and while it's clear that the soul itself isn't a physical thing, it must still exist in some part of the body that controls the other parts. Let's leave aside the other parts or abilities of the soul for now. When it comes to being an animal and being alive, we find that in all creatures that are both alive and animals, there is a single part that makes them both alive and animals. An animal cannot be an animal without being alive. However, something can be alive without being an animal, like plants, which live without feeling anything. It's through sensation that we tell the difference between animals and non-animals.

So, this part of the body that allows for life and being an animal must be the same in number but have different roles, because being alive and being an animal are not exactly the same thing. The organs of the different senses all connect to a single organ where all the senses meet when they work. This organ is located in the middle of the body, between what we call the front and the back (the front is where the senses come in, and the back is the opposite). Also, in all living things, the body is divided into upper and lower parts (even plants have upper and lower parts). This means the part of the body responsible for nutrition must be in the middle of these regions. We call the part where food comes in "the upper part" when we think of it by itself and not compared to the rest of the universe. The "lower part" is where waste is released.

Plants are the opposite of animals in this way. Humans, in particular, because of our upright posture, have our upper parts pointing upwards, like how the universe is structured. Other animals have their upper parts in a middle position. But in plants, because they are rooted in the ground and get their food from the soil, their upper part is always down. The roots of a plant are like the mouth of an animal, as this is where they take in food, whether it's from the earth or from another living thing.

All fully developed animals are divided into three parts: the part that takes in food, the part that releases waste, and the part that is in between. In larger animals, this middle part is called the chest, and in smaller animals, it's something similar. In some animals, this part is more clearly defined than in others. All animals that can move have extra body parts to help with this, such as legs or feet, which allow them to carry their whole body.

It's clear from both observation and reasoning that the source of the body's nourishment is in the middle of these three parts. Many animals can stay alive even when the head or the food container is cut off, as long as the middle part remains attached. This happens in many insects, like wasps and bees. Many other animals, besides insects, can also live after being cut in half as long as the part connected to nutrition remains.

While this middle part of the body is actually one organ, it has the potential to be multiple. These animals are similar to plants in this way. If you cut a plant into sections, each part can keep living, and you can grow multiple trees from one original plant. We will explain later why some plants can't survive when divided, while others can grow from cuttings. But in this way, plants and insects are alike.

The part of the body responsible for nourishment is actually one but has the potential to be many. This is also true for the part responsible for sensation, because the divided parts of these animals can still feel things. However, they can't maintain their structure like plants can because they don't have the organs needed to keep living. Some don't have the ability to grab food, while others can't digest it. They might also be missing other organs.

Animals that can be divided are like several animals growing together, but animals that are more complex are different because their bodies are united in the best possible way. This is why some organs, when divided, still show some sensation because they keep some life in them. For example, tortoises can keep moving even after their heart has been removed.

The same thing happens in both plants and animals. In plants, we see this when they grow from seeds, grafts, and cuttings. Growth from seeds always starts in the middle. All seeds have two halves, and the place where they join is where they attach to the plant, which is a middle part between the two sides. This middle part is where both the root and stem grow. So, the starting point is in the middle between the two. This is especially true for grafts and cuttings, which start growing from buds. The bud is the starting point of the branch and is located in the middle. When we graft a new plant or make a cutting, we either cut the bud or insert the new shoot into it because this is where new growth begins. This shows that growth starts in the middle, between the stem and the root.

In animals with blood, the heart is the first organ to develop. We know this from observing animals when possible. So, in animals without blood, the organ that is like the heart must also develop first. We've already said in our work on animal parts that veins come from the heart, and in animals with blood, the blood is the final nourishment that forms the body parts. This shows that the mouth plays one role in nutrition, and the stomach plays another, but the heart is in control and completes the process. So, in animals with blood, the source of both sensation and nutrition must be in the heart, because the other organs involved in nutrition only help the heart in its work. The main organ is responsible for completing the process, just like how a doctor's goal is to bring about health, not just to focus on smaller tasks.

In all animals with blood, the main organ for sensation is the heart, because this is where the common center for all the senses is located. This is clear for taste and touch because they can be directly connected to the heart. So, the other senses must also lead to the heart, since the heart is where changes start in the other sense organs, while the senses in the head, like taste and touch, are not connected to the heart. Also, if life is always located in the heart, then the source of sensation must also be there. An animal is called "alive" because it can sense things, and we call something an animal because it can feel. In other works, we've explained why some of the senses are connected to the heart and others are in the head. (This is why some people think that sensation comes from the brain.)

If we look at the facts, it's clear that the source of the sensitive soul, along with the part responsible for growth and nutrition, is located in the heart, which is in the middle of the body. This also makes sense from reasoning. In every case, Nature always chooses the best outcome when possible. If both the sensitive and the nutritive principles are located in the middle of the body, the parts responsible for processing food and the parts that receive food will work best. This is because the soul will be close to both, and the central position it holds is the place of control.

The thing that uses a tool and the tool itself must be different. If possible, they should also be separate in space, just like a flute and the hand that plays it. So, if an animal is defined by its ability to sense, this ability must be located in the heart in animals with blood, and in a similar part in animals without blood. In all animals, the body and its parts have some natural warmth, which is why they are warm when alive and cold when dead. This warmth must come from the heart in animals with blood, and from a similar organ in animals without blood. While all parts of the body use their natural heat to process food, the main organ plays the biggest role in this process. This is why life continues even when other parts of the body become cold. But when the warmth in this main organ is gone, death always follows because the heat in all the other parts depends on this organ. The soul is like a fire in this part of the body, which is the heart in animals with blood, and a similar organ in animals without blood. So, life depends on maintaining this heat, and death happens when this heat is destroyed.

It's important to note that fire can stop burning in two ways: either it goes out on its own or something else puts it out. When it stops by itself, we call it exhaustion, and when something else puts it out, we call it extinction. Fire can go out either way from the same cause. When there isn't enough fuel and the heat can't keep burning, the fire dies out. This happens because something blocks digestion and stops the fire from being fed. In other cases, the fire burns out from exhaustion—when heat builds up too much because there's no way to cool down or breathe. In this situation, the heat quickly uses up all its fuel before more can come in. This is why a small fire can be put out by a bigger one, and a candle flame gets swallowed up when placed in a large fire, just like any other burnable material. The bigger fire uses up the fuel before more can be added. Fire is always being created and moving forward, like a river, but it happens so fast we don't notice.

So, if the body's heat needs to be kept steady (which it does to stay alive), there has to be a way to cool down the source of heat. Think of what happens when you cover hot coals in a container. If they stay covered for too long, they burn out. But if you keep lifting the lid and putting it back down quickly, the coals will stay hot for a long time. Piling ashes on a fire also keeps it going, because ashes are porous and allow air to pass through, while also keeping the heat from escaping into the surrounding air. In our work *The Problems*, we've explained why covering a fire makes it go out, while piling ashes on it keeps it burning for a long time.

Everything that is alive has a soul, and as we've said, the soul can't exist without heat in the body. In plants, the natural heat is kept alive by the food they take in and the air around them. Food cools the body when it first enters, just like in humans. When a plant doesn't get food, it produces heat and becomes thirsty. Air, if it doesn't move, becomes hot, but when food enters, it causes movement, which continues until digestion is done, and this cools the body. If the air around the plant is too cold because of the season, the plant withers. Or if, in the heat of summer, the moisture from the ground can't cool the plant, the heat in the plant burns out. When this happens, we say the plants are scorched or burned by the sun. That's why people sometimes put stones or pots of water under the roots of plants to keep them cool.

Some animals live in water, while others live in the air. These environments provide the cooling they need—water for the ones in water, and air for those in the air. We will need to explain more about how exactly this cooling happens.

Afew of the early philosophers talked about breathing. But they either didn't explain why animals breathe, or they gave incorrect explanations, showing they didn't know the facts very well. They also wrongly said that all animals breathe, which isn't true. So, we need to address these points first so we don't seem like we're criticizing those who are no longer alive without reason.

First, it's clear that all animals with lungs breathe. But in some animals, the lungs don't have much blood and are more like sponges, so they don't need to breathe as much. These animals can stay underwater for a long time, relative to their strength. All egg-laying animals, like frogs, have lungs like sponges. Tortoises can also stay underwater for a long time because their lungs don't hold much blood and don't produce much heat. Once their lungs fill with air, the movement of the lungs cools the animal and allows it to stay underwater for a while. However, if an animal holds its breath for too long, it will suffocate, because none of these animals can take in water the way fish do. On the other hand, animals with lungs full of blood need to breathe more because they have more heat. Animals without lungs don't breathe at all.

Democritus and others who wrote about breathing didn't say much about animals without lungs, but they seemed to think that all animals breathe. Anaxagoras and Diogenes both said that all animals breathe, and they tried to explain how fish and oysters breathe. Anaxagoras said that when fish push water through their gills, air forms in their mouths, because there can't be a vacuum. He thought they breathe by taking in this air. Diogenes said that when fish push water out through their gills, they suck air from the water into their mouths because a vacuum is formed in the mouth. He believed there was air in the water.

But these ideas don't work. They only describe part of what's going on and leave out the rest. Breathing involves both inhaling and exhaling air, but these explanations don't say anything about how these animals breathe out. They can't explain it because these animals would have to breathe out through the same passage they breathe in. This would mean that they would have to take water into their mouths while breathing out at the same time. But the air and water would meet and block each other. When the animal pushes water out, it would also have to push out its breath through the mouth or gills. As a result, it would be breathing in and out at the same time, which is impossible. So, if breathing means both inhaling and exhaling air, and these animals can't breathe out, then they can't breathe at all.

Also, the idea that fish breathe by pulling air from the water with their mouths is impossible because they don't have lungs or windpipes. Instead, their stomachs are close to their mouths, so they would have to suck air into their stomachs. If that were true, other animals would do the same, but they don't. Fish also don't do this when they're out of the water, which is obvious. In animals that breathe, you can see movement in the part of the body that pulls in air, but fish don't show any movement in their stomachs, only in their gills. Their gills move both when they are in the water and when they are on land gasping for air. Also, when animals that breathe are drowned, they release air bubbles as the air is forced out, like when a tortoise or frog is held underwater. But this never happens with fish, no matter how we try, because they don't take in air from outside.

If fish really breathed by pulling in air from the water, people should be able to do the same when they are underwater. If fish pull in air through their mouths, why couldn't humans or other animals do that too? But since humans can't do it, neither can fish. Also, why do fish die in the air and gasp as if they are suffocating? It's not because they lack food, and Diogenes' explanation is ridiculous. He says fish die because they take in too much air when out of the water, but in water, they take in just the right amount. But if that were true, land animals should also be able to suffocate from breathing too much air. But that doesn't happen. If all animals breathe, then insects must breathe too. Some insects, like centipedes, seem to live even after being cut into several pieces. How can they breathe when divided, and what organs do they use?

The reason these philosophers gave bad explanations is that they didn't understand the internal organs and didn't believe that everything in nature has a purpose. If they had asked what the purpose of breathing is and thought about the organs involved, like the lungs and gills, they would have figured it out sooner.

Democritus, however, did say that breathing has a purpose. He said it keeps the soul from being pushed out of the body. But he didn't say that nature designed breathing for this purpose. Like the other early philosophers, he didn't reach this level of understanding. He said the soul and heat are the same thing, made up of small, round particles. When the air around us presses on the body and tries to push the soul out, breathing helps prevent this. Democritus thought the air contains many particles of soul and mind, and when we breathe in, these particles enter the body and push back against the pressure, keeping the soul in place.

This is why, he said, life and death are connected to breathing in and out. Death happens when the pressure from the air around us becomes too strong, and the animal can no longer breathe in. At that point, the air can't get in to balance the pressure, and the soul is pushed out of the body. Death, according to him, is the result of the soul being forced out by the pressure of the air around us. Death happens naturally with old age, or unnaturally through violence.

But Democritus didn't explain why death happens or why everything must eventually die. He should have explained whether the cause of death is internal or external, especially since death happens at certain times in life and not others. He also didn't explain where breathing begins or whether its cause is internal or external. It's not true that the air outside controls breathing. The cause of breathing must come from within the body, not from pressure outside. It's also strange to think that the air around us would both squeeze the body and, by entering, expand it at the same time. This is Democritus' theory and how he explains it.

But if our earlier explanation is correct, and not all animals breathe, then Democritus' explanation of death applies only to animals that breathe, not to all animals. And even for animals that breathe, his explanation isn't correct, as we can see from experience. In hot weather, when we get warmer and need to breathe more, we breathe faster. But when the air around us is cold, it shrinks and tightens the body, which slows down breathing. At this time, the outside air should enter the body and cancel out the pressure, but the opposite happens. When we can't breathe out and the heat inside builds up too much, we need to breathe, which means we need to take in air. In hot weather, people breathe faster to cool down, even though Democritus' theory would suggest that they should be adding more heat to their bodies.

The idea from *Timaeus* about breathing, where air is pushed around in the body, doesn't explain how heat is kept in animals other than those that live on land. It also doesn't say if their heat comes from the same or a different source. If breathing only happens in land animals, we should be told why. If other animals also breathe but in a different way, then this form of breathing needs to be explained, assuming all animals breathe.

Also, the explanation seems made up. It says that when hot air leaves the mouth, it pushes the air around it, which then enters the body again through the pores of the skin, filling the place where the warm air came out. This happens because a vacuum (empty space) can't exist. Then, when the air heats up, it leaves the body again through the same route and pushes the warm air back inside through the mouth. They say this process happens continuously when we breathe in and out.

But with this explanation, it would mean we breathe out before we breathe in, which isn't true. The opposite is what really happens, as we can observe. Even though breathing in and out alternates, the last thing we do before death is exhale, so the first act must have been to inhale.

Also, those who explain breathing like this don't say why animals have this function. They make it sound like breathing just happens as part of being alive, but it clearly has control over life and death. When an animal can't breathe, it dies. It's also strange to suggest that the hot air leaving the body is easy to notice, but we can't detect the air entering the lungs and heating up again. It's even more ridiculous to think that breathing involves taking in heat when the opposite is true: we breathe out hot air and take in cool air. When it's hot, we pant because the air coming in isn't cooling us enough, so we have to breathe more frequently.

But we shouldn't think that breathing is for feeding the body like food. Breathing isn't about adding fuel to the body's internal fire, as some have said, with the air acting like food for the flame and then being breathed out. I'll repeat the argument I used earlier against this idea. If that were true, we would see the same thing happening in other animals since they all have body heat. Also, how could breathing create heat? We see that heat comes from food, not air. This theory would also mean that the same passage in the body would be used for taking in food and pushing out waste, but we don't see that happening in other cases.

Empedocles also explained breathing, but he didn't make clear what its purpose is or whether it's universal in all animals. He talked about breathing through the nostrils as if it were the main kind of breathing. But the air that enters through the nostrils also passes through the windpipe and out of the chest, and without the windpipe, the nostrils can't function. Also, if an animal can't breathe through its nose, it's fine. But if it can't breathe through its windpipe, it dies. Nature uses nose breathing for smelling in some animals. The reason why only some animals have it is that, while most animals can smell, they don't all have the same organs for it.

Empedocles also described how breathing works by saying that certain blood vessels hold blood but are not filled with it. These vessels have openings that connect to the air outside the body. The openings are small enough to keep the solid parts of the blood in but large enough for air to pass through. He said that when the blood moves down, air comes in, and this causes inhaling. When the blood moves up, air is pushed out, causing exhaling. He compared this to a water clock, a device used to measure time with water.

Here's how he explained it:

"All things breathe in and out. Their bodies have small tubes that reach the outer edges. These tubes have many channels leading through the nostrils. When the blood moves away, air rushes in. But when the blood moves up, air flows out. This is like a water clock. When a girl puts her hand over the tube and dips it in water, no water enters because the air is trapped. But when she lets the air escape, water rushes in. Just like the water clock, the blood moves, creating space for the air to flow in or out."

That's how he explained breathing. But as we've said, all animals that breathe do so through their windpipe, whether they breathe through their mouth or nose. If he's talking about this kind of breathing, we need to ask how it matches his explanation. The facts seem to go against it. The chest rises like a bellows when we inhale. It makes sense that heat would lift it up and that the blood would gather in the warm area. But the chest sinks back down when we exhale, just like a bellows. The difference is that in breathing, the air comes in and goes out through the same passage, while in a bellows, the air enters and exits through different places.

If Empedocles is only talking about breathing through the nose, he's mistaken. Nose breathing doesn't just involve the nostrils; it also passes through the area near the uvula, at the roof of the mouth. Some of the air goes through the nostrils, and some goes through the mouth, both when we breathe in and when we breathe out.

These are the problems with how other philosophers have explained breathing.

• • •

Section 2

We have already mentioned that life and the presence of a soul involve a certain warmth. Even the process of digesting food, which provides nutrition for animals, doesn't happen without the soul and warmth, because in all cases, digestion is due to heat. That's why the main part of the soul responsible for nutrition must be located in the part of the body where this principle is active. This part is between where food enters and where waste is expelled. In animals without blood, this part doesn't have a name, but in animals with blood, it's called the heart. The blood provides the nourishment from which the animal's organs are made. So, the blood vessels must have the same starting point since they exist to support the blood by serving as its containers. In animals with blood, the heart is where the veins start; they don't pass through it, but instead, they spread out from it, as we can see when we study dissections.

Other abilities of the soul can't exist without the power of nutrition (as explained in the treatise *On the Soul*), and this power depends on natural heat, which Nature has activated by bringing it to life. But fire, as we have already said, can be destroyed in two ways—by going out or burning out. It can be put out by its opposite forces. So, fire can be extinguished by surrounding cold, whether it's in large amounts or spread out (though it happens faster when spread out). This kind of destruction happens by force both in living and non-living things, for cutting an animal apart or freezing it with extreme cold causes death. However, burning out happens when there is too much heat; if the heat is too intense and nothing adds new fuel, the fire will go out because it burns out, not because of cold. So, if it's going to keep going, it needs to be cooled down because cold prevents this kind of burnout.

Some animals live in water, while others live on land. For very small, bloodless animals, the cooling effect of the surrounding water or air is enough to prevent them from burning out due to heat. Since they don't have much heat, they don't need much cold to keep them balanced. This also explains why these animals don't live long, because being small means they have less ability to resist extremes. But some insects live longer, even though they are bloodless like the others, and they have a deep indentation below their middle section to allow cooling through a thinner membrane. These insects are warmer and need more cooling, like bees (some of which live for seven years) and all insects that make a humming noise, such as wasps, beetles, and crickets. They make a sound that's like panting by using air, as the air inside them causes a rising and falling movement that creates friction against the membrane. The way they move this area is similar to how the lungs move in animals that breathe, or how gills move in fish. What happens is like when an animal that breathes air is suffocated by blocking its mouth, causing the lungs to make a similar rising and falling movement. In these animals, this internal movement isn't enough for cooling, but in insects, it is. By creating friction against the membrane, they make the humming sound, as we said, similar to how children make sounds by blowing through a reed covered by a thin membrane. This is also how crickets make their songs; they have more heat and a deeper indentation at the waist, while those that don't make noise have no such indentation.

Animals that have blood and lungs, but whose lungs have little blood and are spongy, can sometimes live for a long time without breathing, because the lung, with its small amount of blood or liquid, can rise very high, and its own movement can keep cooling the body for a long time. But eventually, this is not enough, and the animal dies from suffocation if it doesn't breathe, as we've already mentioned. Exhaustion due to a lack of cooling is called suffocation, and anything that dies this way is said to be suffocated.

We've already said that insects don't breathe like other animals, and we can observe this in small creatures like flies and bees, which can move around in a liquid for a long time as long as it's not too hot or cold. However, animals with little strength tend to breathe more often. These animals die from what we call suffocation when their stomach fills up and the heat in their middle part is lost. This is also why they can revive after being in ashes for some time.

Among water animals, those without blood can live longer in air than those with blood, like fish. Since they have a small amount of heat, the air can cool them for a long time, as we see in animals like crabs and octopuses. However, the air is not enough to keep them alive because they don't have enough heat. Many fish can also live in the soil, though they stay still, and they can be found by digging. All animals that don't have lungs or have bloodless lungs need less cooling.

Regarding bloodless animals, we've explained that some rely on the surrounding air and others on fluids to maintain life. But for animals with blood and a heart, all those with lungs take in air and cool themselves by breathing in and out. All animals that give birth to live young and do so inside their bodies (unlike the Selachia, which give birth outside) have lungs, as do oviparous animals, such as birds and scaly animals like tortoises, lizards, and snakes. In the first group, the lungs are filled with blood, but in most of the latter, the lungs are spongy. So, they breathe less often, as we've said before. This function is also found in animals that live in water, like water snakes, frogs, crocodiles, and turtles, whether they live in the sea or on land, as well as in seals.

All these animals give birth on land and sleep on land, or when they sleep in water, they keep their heads above the surface to breathe. But animals with gills cool themselves by taking in water; this includes Selachia and other animals without legs. Fish have no legs, and their fins are named for their resemblance to wings. However, one animal with legs, the tadpole, has gills.

No animal has both lungs and gills, and the reason is that lungs are made for cooling through air (their name, "pneumon," seems to come from their function as a container for breath), while gills are for cooling through water. Since one tool is enough for one purpose, Nature doesn't make unnecessary organs. So, some animals have gills, others have lungs, but none have both.

Every animal needs food to live and cooling to prevent death. Nature uses the same organ for both tasks. For example, in some animals, the tongue is used both to taste food and for speaking. In animals with lungs, the mouth is used to break down food and to let air in and out. In animals without lungs or that don't breathe, the mouth is just used to break down food, while in animals that need cooling, gills are made for this purpose.

We'll explain later how these organs produce cooling. But to make sure food doesn't interfere with breathing, both respiring animals and those that take in water have a similar system. When they breathe, they don't take in food, because food, whether liquid or dry, could get into the windpipe and cause suffocation by blocking the lungs. The windpipe is located in front of the esophagus, through which food goes into the stomach. In blooded quadrupeds, there is a lid called the epiglottis over the windpipe. In birds and egg-laying quadrupeds, this covering is missing, but they close their windpipes by contracting them. When swallowing food, birds contract the windpipe while mammals close the epiglottis. Once the food has passed, the epiglottis is raised, or the windpipe expands, allowing air to enter and cool the body. In animals with gills, water is expelled first, then food enters the mouth. They don't have a windpipe, so they aren't harmed by liquids entering their windpipe, only by liquids entering the stomach. This is why these animals quickly expel water and grab their food. Their teeth are sharp and often arranged like a saw because they can't chew their food.

Among water animals, cetaceans, like dolphins and whales, may seem puzzling, but they can be explained. Examples of these animals include dolphins, whales, and others with blowholes. They don't have legs but do have lungs, even though they live in water. They have lungs for cooling, as we mentioned, but they don't take in water to cool themselves. Instead, they cool down by breathing because they have lungs. That's why they sleep with their heads out of the water, and dolphins even snore. If they get caught in nets, they die quickly from suffocation because they can't breathe. So, they can be seen coming to the surface to breathe. Since they need to eat in the water, they take in water and expel it through their blowholes, just as fish expel water through their gills. The blowhole is placed in front of the brain, where it releases the water without touching any of the blood-filled organs.

Mollusks and crustaceans, like crabs, also take in water for the same reason. These animals don't need cooling because they don't have much heat and are bloodless. The surrounding water cools them enough. But when they eat, they take in water, and they have to expel it to avoid swallowing it along with the food. Crustaceans, like crabs and lobsters, expel water through the folds beside their hairy parts, while cuttlefish and octopuses use the hollow above their heads. There's a more detailed explanation of these animals in *The History of Animals*.

This explains why animals take in water for cooling and how those that live in water must eat in it as well.

We must now explain how cooling happens in animals that breathe and those with gills. We've already said that all animals with lungs breathe. The reason some creatures have lungs, and those that do need to breathe, is that higher animals have more heat. Since they have a higher soul and nature than plants, they need this. Animals with more blood and warmth in their lungs tend to be larger, and the animal with the purest and most abundant blood in the lungs is the most upright—this is man. The reason man alone stands with his upper part directed toward the upper part of the universe is that he has such lungs.

So, the lungs must be considered an essential part of the animal's nature, both in humans and in other animals.

This is the purpose of cooling. As for the cause behind this, we must believe that nature made animals this way, just as it made many other animals with different compositions. Some animals have more earth in their makeup, like plants, while others, like aquatic animals, have more water. Winged and land animals have more air and fire, respectively. Each thing exists in the region that suits the element most abundant in its composition.

Empedocles was wrong when he said that animals with the most warmth and fire live in water to balance the heat in their bodies. He thought that since they lack cold and fluid, living in water keeps them alive, as water has less heat than air. But it makes no sense that water animals would all originate on land and then move to the water, especially since most of them have no legs. Yet, he said that they were first created on land and then moved to the water. But it's clear that water animals aren't warmer than land animals, as some have no blood at all, and others have very little.

We've already discussed what kinds of animals should be considered warm and what kinds cold. While

Empedocles' idea has some logic, his explanation is wrong. A condition that is too extreme is balanced by its opposite, but the best way for an animal's body to stay healthy is to be in an environment similar to its own nature. There's a difference between what an animal is made of and the condition of that material. For example, if nature made something out of wax or ice, it wouldn't be kept safe in a hot place because heat would quickly destroy it, as heat melts what cold freezes. Likewise, something made of salt or nitre wouldn't be placed in water because water would dissolve it, as its structure depends on being dry and warm.

So, if all bodies are made of wet and dry materials, it makes sense that things made mostly of wet and cold elements would live in liquid environments. And if they are cold, they would exist in cold places, while things made mostly of dry elements would be found on land. Trees, for instance, don't grow in water but on dry land. But according to Empedocles' theory, they should live in water because they are so dry, just like things that are very fiery. They would move to water, not because of the cold, but because of its fluid nature.

In reality, the natural state of materials is suited to the regions they exist in. Liquids belong in liquid environments, dry things on land, and warm things in the air. However, in terms of a body's condition, a cold environment helps balance out too much heat, while a warm one helps balance too much cold. The region around the animal adjusts the excess condition in its body. The regions where things live and the changing seasons also help fix such imbalances. But while a body's condition can be the opposite of its surroundings, the material that makes up the body cannot be. This explains why some animals are aquatic and others are terrestrial, and why some have lungs while others do not. It's not because of the amount of heat in their bodies, as Empedocles claimed.

The reason animals with lungs, especially those with lungs full of blood, breathe air is because the lungs are spongy and full of tubes. The lungs also have more blood than any other organ. All animals with blood-filled lungs need to cool down quickly because they don't have much room for changes in their body heat. The air needs to get through the entire lung because of the large amount of blood and heat it holds. Air can easily do this because it's light and can spread everywhere quickly, allowing it to cool down the body. Water, on the other hand, can't do this as easily.

This explains why animals with blood-filled lungs breathe more often—the more heat they have, the more cooling they need. Also, air can easily reach the source of heat in the heart.

To understand how the heart connects to the lungs through passages, we should look at dissections and the information in the *History of Animals*. The main reason animals need cooling is that the soul and fire come together in the heart. Breathing is how animals with lungs and a heart cool themselves. But for animals like fish, which live in water and don't have lungs, cooling happens through the gills using water. If you want to see how the heart connects to the gills, you need to look at dissections, and for more details, refer to *Natural History*. For now, we can sum it up like this.

It might seem like the heart is in a different position in land animals and fish, but the position is actually the same. The tip of the heart points in the direction the animal tilts its head. In fish, the tip of the heart points toward the mouth, since they don't tilt their heads the same way land animals do. From the tip of the heart, a large, strong tube runs to the center where all the gills meet. This is the biggest tube, but there are others on either side of the heart that go to each gill. Water constantly flows through the gills, cooling the heart.

In the same way fish move their gills, animals that breathe raise and lower their chest as they inhale and exhale. If there isn't enough fresh air, or if the air isn't replaced, they suffocate because the air, after touching the blood, heats up quickly. The heat from the blood cancels out the cooling effect, and when animals can't move their lungs (or fish can't move their gills) due to sickness or old age, they die.

Being born and dying are common to all animals, but there are different ways these things happen. There are different types of death, though they all have something in common. There is violent death, caused by something outside the body, and natural death, caused by something inside the body, built into the way the body is made. It's not something that comes from outside. For plants, this is called withering; for animals, it's called aging. Death and decay happen to everything that is fully developed, though it can also happen to things that aren't fully developed, like eggs or seeds before they sprout roots.

Death always happens due to a loss of heat, and in fully developed creatures, this happens when heat runs out in the organ that is the source of the creature's essential life. As we've said, this organ is located between the upper and lower parts of the body. In plants, it's between the root and the stem, and in animals with blood, it's the heart. In bloodless animals, it's the equivalent part of their body. Some animals have many potential sources of life, though they actually have only one. This explains why some insects can keep living even when they are cut in half, and why even some animals with blood can live for a long time after their heart is removed. For example, tortoises can still move their legs as long as they have their shell, which is due to their naturally weaker constitution, as we see in insects too.

Life ends when the heat that sustains it is no longer cooled properly. As I've said before, the heat burns itself up. So, when the lungs in one type of animal, or the gills in another, dry out over time, they become hard and earthy, unable to move. They can't expand or contract anymore. Eventually, the fire goes out due to exhaustion.

This is why even a small disturbance can cause death in old age. There isn't much heat left because most of it has been used up over the long life. Any extra strain on the body can quickly extinguish what's left. It's like the heart contains a small, weak flame that can easily be put out by the slightest movement. This is why death in old age is painless—there's no need for a violent event to cause it, and the soul departs quietly without feeling anything. Diseases that harden the lungs, such as tumors or excess heat from fevers, speed up breathing because the lungs can't move much either up or down. When the lungs can't move at all, breathing stops, and death follows.

Being born is when an animal first shares in the life-giving soul through warmth, and life is the process of keeping this connection. Youth is the time when the organ for cooling grows, old age is when it starts to decay, and the time in between is the prime of life.

A violent death happens when the vital heat is put out or burns out (both can cause death), while natural death happens when the heat runs out over time and life ends. For plants, this is called withering; for animals, it's called dying. In old age, death is caused by the body's inability to keep cooling itself due to the passage of time. This is our explanation of birth, life, and death, and why they happen in animals.

It is clear why animals that breathe air suffocate in water, and why fish suffocate in air. For fish, water provides the cooling they need, while for animals that breathe air, the air does the same. When either is taken away by a change in their environment, the function is lost.

We must also explain why gills and lungs move the way they do, and how this movement allows air or water to come in and go out. Here's how these organs are structured.

There are three things related to the heart that might seem similar but are actually different: palpitation, pulsation, and respiration.

Palpitation happens when the hot substance in the heart rushes together due to the cooling effect of waste products. This happens in conditions like spasms and other illnesses. It also occurs when you're scared, because when you're afraid, the upper parts of your body become cold, and the hot substance retreats to the heart. This causes the heart to palpitate because the heat is squeezed into such a small space that sometimes life is extinguished, and animals can die from fear and the disturbance it causes.

The constant beating of the heart is similar to the throbbing of an abscess. However, an abscess is painful because the blood changes in an unnatural way, and the throbbing continues until the matter inside is discharged. This process is similar to boiling, where heat turns liquid into vapor and expands it. But in an abscess, if nothing evaporates, the liquid thickens, and the process ends in the formation of pus. In boiling, it ends with the liquid escaping from the container.

In the heart, the beating is caused by heat expanding the liquid, which comes from food. This happens when the liquid rises to the outer wall of the heart and continues without stopping. There is always a constant flow of liquid that turns into blood, and the heart is where blood is first formed. We can see this in the early stages of life, as the heart contains blood before the veins become clear. This is why young people have faster pulses than older people, as there's more vapor being produced in the young.

All veins pulse at the same time because they are connected to the heart. Since the heart always beats, the veins also beat continuously and in sync with the heart.

So, palpitation is the heart's reaction to being squeezed by cold, while pulsation is caused by the heated liquid turning into vapor.

Respiration happens when the hot substance, which is the source of nutrition, grows. This part of the body needs more nutrition than other parts because it feeds them. As it grows, it makes the organ expand. This organ is built like a pair of bellows, similar to those used by blacksmiths. The heart and lungs have a similar shape. This structure must be double because the source of nutrition needs to be at the center of the natural forces.

As the organ expands, it causes the surrounding parts to rise. We can see this happen when people breathe. They lift their chest because the part inside the chest expands the same way. When this part expands, air rushes in like it would in bellows. The air is cold, so it cools the heat by reducing the excess fire. When the organ shrinks, the air that entered is pushed back out. When air enters, it's cold, but when it exits, it's warm because it has been in contact with the heat in the organ. This is especially true for animals with lungs full of blood. The lung has many tubes with blood vessels next to them, so it seems like the whole lung is full of blood. The movement of air inward is called respiration, and the movement outward is called expiration. This process continues for as long as the animal lives, as the organ keeps moving constantly. Life is tied to this constant movement of air in and out.

The movement of gills in fish happens in the same way. When the hot substance in the blood rises, the gills rise too and let water pass through. When the heat is cooled and flows back to the heart, the gills contract and push the water out. As the heat in the heart rises and then cools, this process repeats. So, just as breathing is tied to life and death in air-breathing animals, water entering and exiting is tied to life and death in fish.

We have now covered life, death, and related topics. But health and disease also deserve the attention of scientists, not just doctors, when it comes to understanding their causes. It's important to recognize the difference between the work of scientists and that of physicians, although they overlap in some ways. Doctors who are well-educated often mention natural science and claim that their methods come from it. On the other hand, the best scientists often take their studies so far that they end up discussing medical principles too.

•••

On Life and Death

Aristotle's Inquiry into the Nature of Existence

A Modern Translation

Adapted for the Contemporary Reader

Aristotle

Translated by Tim Zengerink

Introduction

Ancient Greece was a civilization famous for its great contributions to philosophy, politics, art, and science. It thrived from the 8th century BCE until the Roman Empire started to decline. Greece's city-states, especially Athens, were the heart of culture and intellectual thought. This was the time when democracy began, impressive buildings like the Parthenon were built, and famous playwrights like Sophocles and Euripides produced their works. The Greeks' curiosity about the world around them laid the foundation for Western philosophy. Thinkers like Socrates, Plato, and later Aristotle, pushed the limits of what people understood about the world.

Greek society was deeply connected to theism, which focused on a large group of gods and goddesses who were believed to control every part of life. But this system did not prevent people from exploring new ideas. In fact, it coexisted with a growing interest in finding logical explanations for nature and human

life. Intellectuals would often debate and discuss these ideas in public places like the Agora. Aristotle grew up in this dynamic environment, learning from earlier philosophers, and later challenging and expanding their ideas.

Aristotle's Life

Aristotle was born in 384 BCE in a small town called Stagira, located in northern Greece. His father, Nicomachus, was a doctor for King Amyntas of Macedon, and this allowed Aristotle to be around the Macedonian royal court from a young age. When his parents passed away, Aristotle was sent to Athens at the age of 17 to pursue his education. Athens was the center of intellectual life in Greece, and Aristotle joined Plato's Academy, which was the most respected school of the time. The Academy was a place where students discussed everything from ethics to science. Although Aristotle learned a lot from Plato, he did not always agree with him, especially when it came to metaphysics, which deals with the nature of reality.

After spending almost 20 years at the Academy, Aristotle left Athens around 347 BCE after Plato's death. He traveled around different cities in Greece, continuing to study and learn. In 343 BCE, he was

invited to the court of King Philip II of Macedon, where he became the tutor of Philip's son, Alexander, who would later become known as Alexander the Great. Aristotle taught Alexander about philosophy, ethics, politics, and science. Aristotle's influence is visible in Alexander's leadership style, which showed respect for knowledge and strategic thinking.

After teaching Alexander, Aristotle returned to Athens in 335 BCE, where he opened his own school called the Lyceum. Unlike Plato's Academy, the Lyceum focused more on recording knowledge and observing nature. Aristotle and his students performed research, studied animals, and took notes on what they observed. The Lyceum became a major center of learning, and it rivaled Plato's Academy. This is also where Aristotle wrote many of his famous works.

Later in life, after the death of Alexander in 323 BCE, the political climate in Athens became difficult for Aristotle because of his connections to the Macedonian court. Accused of disrespecting the gods, Aristotle decided to leave Athens. He fled to Chalcis, where he passed away in 322 BCE. Even though he had to leave Athens, his legacy lived on through his many writings and the influence of his school, the Lyceum.

Aristotle's Impact on Western Thought

No figure looms larger over the development of Western philosophy and science than Aristotle. A student of Plato and tutor to Alexander the Great, he unified logic, ethics, politics, rhetoric, and metaphysics into a coherent system that shaped intellectual inquiry for centuries. Although his writings reflect the best knowledge of his era, they also reveal a distinctive way of understanding the world—one that balances observation with rigorous logical analysis. Over time, this method has profoundly influenced everything from political theory to modern scientific methodology.

Aristotle approached knowledge as an interconnected whole, seeing each field of study as a vital path toward truth. While many earlier thinkers focused on abstract concepts, he emphasized direct observation of the natural world. By systematically examining and classifying what he saw, Aristotle laid the groundwork for the empirical methods now central to modern science. Although our understanding of nature has evolved, his legacy endures in today's emphasis on evidence-based research.

Logic: The Foundation of Rational Inquiry

Often hailed as the "father of formal logic," Aristotle introduced a system of reasoning that shaped intellectual discourse for over two millennia. In works like the Organon, he analyzed how valid conclusions are drawn from premises and introduced syllogisms—deductive arguments that became standard tools in philosophy, theology, and science. Even contemporary logic, despite its modern mathematical and symbolic advancements, can trace many of its core principles back to Aristotle's pioneering analyses.

Metaphysics: Exploring the Nature of Reality

Aristotle's Metaphysics offered one of the earliest comprehensive explorations of existence at its most fundamental level. There, he described the nature of "being qua being" and introduced the concepts of potentiality and actuality to explain how things change and develop. These ideas deeply influenced medieval scholastics—both Christian and Islamic—who integrated Aristotelian reasoning into their theological frameworks. Today, discussions about consciousness, identity, and free will still reference these Aristotelian notions.

Ethics and the Pursuit of the Good Life

In the Nicomachean Ethics, Aristotle proposed that the ultimate aim of human life is eudaimonia, often translated as "happiness" or "flourishing." He argued that we achieve this through virtue, developed by cultivating good habits guided by reason. His famous Doctrine of the Mean asserts that moral virtue resides between two extremes—for instance, courage lies between recklessness and cowardice. This focus on character formation has profoundly shaped the tradition known as "virtue ethics," influencing modern debates on moral education, personal development, and what it means to live well.

Politics: The Role of the Individual in the City-State

Aristotle's practical approach to ethics naturally extended into political theory. In Politics, he explored various forms of government—monarchy, aristocracy, oligarchy, democracy—and weighed their merits and pitfalls. For Aristotle, a well-ordered polis (city-state) exists not merely for survival or trade but to enable its citizens to live virtuous, fulfilling lives. His conviction that ethics

and politics are intertwined remains influential, informing contemporary discussions on citizenship, governance, and justice.

Rhetoric: The Art of Persuasion

In his treatise Rhetoric, Aristotle examined how persuasion works, detailing how arguments must appeal to ethos (credibility), pathos (emotion), and logos (logic). This clear framework for effective communication continues to guide public speakers, legal advocates, and writers. From ancient courtroom orations to modern political campaigns, Aristotelian rhetoric underpins many of the strategies people use to sway audiences and shape public opinion.

Beyond these core subjects, Aristotle made significant contributions to biology, physics, psychology, and aesthetics. In the Poetics, for example, he investigated why humans respond so powerfully to tragic drama, pioneering the concept of catharsis—the emotional release that audiences feel through art. Throughout the medieval period, thinkers like Thomas Aquinas integrated Aristotle's theories into Christian theology, while Islamic philosophers such as Avicenna and Averroes preserved, interpreted, and expanded upon his works.

Across centuries of reinterpretation and debate, Aristotle remains a living voice in contemporary thought. His insistence on systematically gathering evidence and connecting it to logical principles laid the foundation for what we now recognize as the scientific method. His inquiries into human flourishing, civic responsibility, and the nature of argument continue to spark discussion and inspire new research. From personal ethics to societal organization, Aristotle's ideas help us frame enduring questions about how best to live, learn, and understand reality.

In sum, Aristotle stands as a foundational pillar of Western thought. He bridged abstract theorizing and practical inquiry, bequeathing a vision of knowledge that values both reason and experience. From ethics and politics to science and art, his ideas have been woven into countless intellectual traditions. Even today, as we grapple with questions of morality, governance, and truth, we walk in the footsteps of an ancient thinker whose breadth of insight and depth of analysis continue to guide our pursuit of wisdom.

Final Thoughts

By preserving Aristotle's legacy, we protect the intellectual depth and rigor that defined his way

of understanding the world. His systematic way of asking questions, his classification of knowledge, and his ethical theories are still relevant today, providing a model for critical thinking across many subjects. This preservation is important not just for philosophy students but for anyone interested in the foundations of human thought and the development of ideas that shape the world we live in.

One of the difficulties in studying Aristotle's work is that his ideas and language are complex. Translating these works into our modern language is a key step in making his profound insights easier for more people to understand. By putting his ideas into today's language, more readers can engage with his thoughts, even if they don't have a background in classical studies. Making Aristotle's work accessible means adapting them to modern ways of thinking without losing their original depth. This helps bridge the gap between ancient and modern readers, making sure Aristotle's work stays relevant.

Section 1

We now need to talk about youth, old age, life, and death. We will probably also need to explain the causes of breathing, since living and dying sometimes depend on it.

We have already explained the soul in detail elsewhere, and while it's clear that the soul itself isn't a physical thing, it must still exist in some part of the body that controls the other parts. Let's leave aside the other parts or abilities of the soul for now. When it comes to being an animal and being alive, we find that in all creatures that are both alive and animals, there is a single part that makes them both alive and animals. An animal cannot be an animal without being alive. However, something can be alive without being an animal, like plants, which live without feeling anything. It's through sensation that we tell the difference between animals and non-animals.

So, this part of the body that allows for life and being an animal must be the same in number but have different roles, because being alive and being an animal are not exactly the same thing. The organs of the different senses all connect to a single organ where all the senses meet when they work. This organ is located in the middle of the body, between what we call the front and the back (the front is where the senses come in, and the back is the opposite). Also, in all living things, the body is divided into upper and lower parts (even plants have upper and lower parts). This means the part of the body responsible for nutrition must be in the middle of these regions. We call the part where food comes in "the upper part" when we think of it by itself and not compared to the rest of the universe. The "lower part" is where waste is released.

Plants are the opposite of animals in this way. Humans, in particular, because of our upright posture, have our upper parts pointing upwards, like how the universe is structured. Other animals have their upper parts in a middle position. But in plants, because they are rooted in the ground and get their food from the soil, their upper part is always down. The roots of a plant are like the mouth of an animal, as this is where they take in food, whether it's from the earth or from another living thing.

All fully developed animals are divided into three parts: the part that takes in food, the part that releases waste, and the part that is in between. In larger animals, this middle part is called the chest, and in smaller animals, it's something similar. In some animals, this part is more clearly defined than in others. All animals that can move have extra body parts to help with this, such as legs or feet, which allow them to carry their whole body.

It's clear from both observation and reasoning that the source of the body's nourishment is in the middle of these three parts. Many animals can stay alive even when the head or the food container is cut off, as long as the middle part remains attached. This happens in many insects, like wasps and bees. Many other animals, besides insects, can also live after being cut in half as long as the part connected to nutrition remains.

While this middle part of the body is actually one organ, it has the potential to be multiple. These animals are similar to plants in this way. If you cut a plant into sections, each part can keep living, and you can grow multiple trees from one original plant. We will explain later why some plants can't survive when divided, while others can grow from cuttings. But in this way, plants and insects are alike.

The part of the body responsible for nourishment is actually one but has the potential to be many. This is also true for the part responsible for sensation, because the divided parts of these animals can still feel things. However, they can't maintain their structure like plants can because they don't have the organs needed to keep living. Some don't have the ability to grab food, while others can't digest it. They might also be missing other organs.

Animals that can be divided are like several animals growing together, but animals that are more complex are different because their bodies are united in the best possible way. This is why some organs, when divided, still show some sensation because they keep some life in them. For example, tortoises can keep moving even after their heart has been removed.

The same thing happens in both plants and animals. In plants, we see this when they grow from seeds, grafts, and cuttings. Growth from seeds always starts in the middle. All seeds have two halves, and the place where they join is where they attach to the plant, which is a middle part between the two sides. This middle part is where both the root and stem grow. So, the starting point is in the middle between the two. This is especially true for grafts and cuttings, which start growing from buds. The bud is the starting point of the branch and is located in the middle. When we graft a new plant or make a cutting, we either cut the bud or insert the new shoot into it because this is where new growth begins. This shows that growth starts in the middle, between the stem and the root.

In animals with blood, the heart is the first organ to develop. We know this from observing animals when possible. So, in animals without blood, the organ that is like the heart must also develop first. We've already said in our work on animal parts that veins come from the heart, and in animals with blood, the blood is the final nourishment that forms the body parts. This shows that the mouth plays one role in nutrition, and the stomach plays another, but the heart is in control and completes the process. So, in animals with blood, the source of both sensation and nutrition must be in the heart, because the other organs involved in nutrition only help the heart in its work. The main organ is responsible for completing the process, just like how a doctor's goal is to bring about health, not just to focus on smaller tasks.

In all animals with blood, the main organ for sensation is the heart, because this is where the common center for all the senses is located. This is clear for taste and touch because they can be directly connected to the heart. So, the other senses must also lead to the heart, since the heart is where changes start in the other sense organs, while the senses in the head, like taste and touch, are not connected to the heart. Also, if life is always located in the heart, then the source of sensation must also be there. An animal is called "alive" because it can sense things, and we call something an animal because it can feel. In other works, we've explained why some of the senses are connected to the heart and others are in the head. (This is why some people think that sensation comes from the brain.)

If we look at the facts, it's clear that the source of the sensitive soul, along with the part responsible for growth and nutrition, is located in the heart, which is in the middle of the body. This also makes sense from reasoning. In every case, Nature always chooses the best outcome when possible. If both the sensitive and the nutritive principles are located in the middle of the body, the parts responsible for processing food and the parts that receive food will work best. This is because the soul will be close to both, and the central position it holds is the place of control.

The thing that uses a tool and the tool itself must be different. If possible, they should also be separate in space, just like a flute and the hand that plays it. So, if an animal is defined by its ability to sense, this ability must be located in the heart in animals with blood, and in a similar part in animals without blood. In all animals, the body and its parts have some natural warmth, which is why they are warm when alive and cold when dead. This warmth must come from the heart in animals with blood, and from a similar organ in animals without blood. While all parts of the body use their natural heat to process food, the main organ plays the biggest role in this process. This is why life continues even when other parts of the body become cold. But when the warmth in this main organ is gone, death always follows because the heat in all the other parts depends on this organ. The soul is like a fire in this part of the body, which is the heart in animals with blood, and a similar organ in animals without blood. So, life depends on maintaining this heat, and death happens when this heat is destroyed.

It's important to note that fire can stop burning in two ways: either it goes out on its own or something else puts it out. When it stops by itself, we call it exhaustion, and when something else puts it out, we call it extinction. Fire can go out either way from the same cause. When there isn't enough fuel and the heat can't keep burning, the fire dies out. This happens because something blocks digestion and stops the fire from being fed. In other cases, the fire burns out from exhaustion—when heat builds up too much because there's no way to cool down or breathe. In this situation, the heat quickly uses up all its fuel before more can come in. This is why a small fire can be put out by a bigger one, and a candle flame gets swallowed up when placed in a large fire, just like any other burnable material. The bigger fire uses up the fuel before more can be added. Fire is always being created and moving forward, like a river, but it happens so fast we don't notice.

So, if the body's heat needs to be kept steady (which it does to stay alive), there has to be a way to cool down the source of heat. Think of what happens when you cover hot coals in a container. If they stay covered for too long, they burn out. But if you keep lifting the lid and putting it back down quickly, the coals will stay hot for a long time. Piling ashes on a fire also keeps it going, because ashes are porous and allow air to pass through, while also keeping the heat from escaping into the surrounding air. In our work *The Problems*, we've explained why covering a fire makes it go out, while piling ashes on it keeps it burning for a long time.

Everything that is alive has a soul, and as we've said, the soul can't exist without heat in the body. In plants, the natural heat is kept alive by the food they take in and the air around them. Food cools the body when it first enters, just like in humans. When a plant doesn't get food, it produces heat and becomes thirsty. Air, if it doesn't move, becomes hot, but when food enters, it causes movement, which continues until digestion is done, and this cools the body. If the air around the plant is too cold because of the season, the plant withers. Or if, in the heat of summer, the moisture from the ground can't cool the plant, the heat in the plant burns out. When this happens, we say the plants are scorched or burned by the sun. That's why people sometimes put stones or pots of water under the roots of plants to keep them cool.

Some animals live in water, while others live in the air. These environments provide the cooling they need—water for the ones in water, and air for those in the air. We will need to explain more about how exactly this cooling happens.

Afew of the early philosophers talked about breathing. But they either didn't explain why animals breathe, or they gave incorrect explanations, showing they didn't know the facts very well. They also wrongly said that all animals breathe, which isn't true. So, we need to address these points first so we don't seem like we're criticizing those who are no longer alive without reason.

First, it's clear that all animals with lungs breathe. But in some animals, the lungs don't have much blood and are more like sponges, so they don't need to breathe as much. These animals can stay underwater for a long time, relative to their strength. All egg-laying animals, like frogs, have lungs like sponges. Tortoises can also stay underwater for a long time because their lungs don't hold much blood and don't produce much heat. Once their lungs fill with air, the movement of the lungs cools the animal and allows it to stay underwater for a while. However, if an animal holds its breath for too long, it will suffocate, because none of these animals can take in water the way fish do. On the other hand, animals with lungs full of blood need to breathe more because they have more heat. Animals without lungs don't breathe at all.

Democritus and others who wrote about breathing didn't say much about animals without lungs, but they seemed to think that all animals breathe. Anaxagoras and Diogenes both said that all animals breathe, and they tried to explain how fish and oysters breathe. Anaxagoras said that when fish push water through their gills, air forms in their mouths, because there can't be a vacuum. He thought they breathe by taking in this air. Diogenes said that when fish push water out through their gills, they suck air from the water into their mouths because a vacuum is formed in the mouth. He believed there was air in the water.

But these ideas don't work. They only describe part of what's going on and leave out the rest. Breathing involves both inhaling and exhaling air, but these explanations don't say anything about how these animals breathe out. They can't explain it because these animals would have to breathe out through the same passage they breathe in. This would mean that they would have to take water into their mouths while breathing out at the same time. But the air and water would meet and block each other. When the animal pushes water out, it would also have to push out its breath through the mouth or gills. As a result, it would be breathing in and out at the same time, which is impossible. So, if breathing means both inhaling and exhaling air, and these animals can't breathe out, then they can't breathe at all.

Also, the idea that fish breathe by pulling air from the water with their mouths is impossible because they don't have lungs or windpipes. Instead, their stomachs are close to their mouths, so they would have to suck air into their stomachs. If that were true, other animals would do the same, but they don't. Fish also don't do this when they're out of the water, which is obvious. In animals that breathe, you can see movement in the part of the body that pulls in air, but fish don't show any movement in their stomachs, only in their gills. Their gills move both when they are in the water and when they are on land gasping for air. Also, when animals that breathe are drowned, they release air bubbles as the air is forced out, like when a tortoise or frog is held underwater. But this never happens with fish, no matter how we try, because they don't take in air from outside.

If fish really breathed by pulling in air from the water, people should be able to do the same when they are underwater. If fish pull in air through their mouths, why couldn't humans or other animals do that too? But since humans can't do it, neither can fish. Also, why do fish die in the air and gasp as if they are suffocating? It's not because they lack food, and Diogenes' explanation is ridiculous. He says fish die because they take in too much air when out of the water, but in water, they take in just the right amount. But if that were true, land animals should also be able to suffocate from breathing too much air. But that doesn't happen. If all animals breathe, then insects must breathe too. Some insects, like centipedes, seem to live even after being cut into several pieces. How can they breathe when divided, and what organs do they use?

The reason these philosophers gave bad explanations is that they didn't understand the internal organs and didn't believe that everything in nature has a purpose. If they had asked what the purpose of breathing is and thought about the organs involved, like the lungs and gills, they would have figured it out sooner.

Democritus, however, did say that breathing has a purpose. He said it keeps the soul from being pushed out of the body. But he didn't say that nature designed breathing for this purpose. Like the other early philosophers, he didn't reach this level of understanding. He said the soul and heat are the same thing, made up of small, round particles. When the air around us presses on the body and tries to push the soul out, breathing helps prevent this. Democritus thought the air contains many particles of soul and mind, and when we breathe in, these particles enter the body and push back against the pressure, keeping the soul in place.

This is why, he said, life and death are connected to breathing in and out. Death happens when the pressure from the air around us becomes too strong, and the animal can no longer breathe in. At that point, the air can't get in to balance the pressure, and the soul is pushed out of the body. Death, according to him, is the result of the soul being forced out by the pressure of the air around us. Death happens naturally with old age, or unnaturally through violence.

But Democritus didn't explain why death happens or why everything must eventually die. He should have explained whether the cause of death is internal or external, especially since death happens at certain times in life and not others. He also didn't explain where breathing begins or whether its cause is internal or external. It's not true that the air outside controls breathing. The cause of breathing must come from within the body, not from pressure outside. It's also strange to think that the air around us would both squeeze the body and, by entering, expand it at the same time. This is Democritus' theory and how he explains it.

But if our earlier explanation is correct, and not all animals breathe, then Democritus' explanation of death applies only to animals that breathe, not to all animals. And even for animals that breathe, his explanation isn't correct, as we can see from experience. In hot weather, when we get warmer and need to breathe more, we breathe faster. But when the air around us is cold, it shrinks and tightens the body, which slows down breathing. At this time, the outside air should enter the body and cancel out the pressure, but the opposite happens. When we can't breathe out and the heat inside builds up too much, we need to breathe, which means we need to take in air. In hot weather, people breathe faster to cool down, even though Democritus' theory would suggest that they should be adding more heat to their bodies.

The idea from *Timaeus* about breathing, where air is pushed around in the body, doesn't explain how heat is kept in animals other than those that live on land. It also doesn't say if their heat comes from the same or a different source. If breathing only happens in land animals, we should be told why. If other animals also breathe but in a different way, then this form of breathing needs to be explained, assuming all animals breathe.

Also, the explanation seems made up. It says that when hot air leaves the mouth, it pushes the air around it, which then enters the body again through the pores of the skin, filling the place where the warm air came out. This happens because a vacuum (empty space) can't exist. Then, when the air heats up, it leaves the body again through the same route and pushes the warm air back inside through the mouth. They say this process happens continuously when we breathe in and out.

But with this explanation, it would mean we breathe out before we breathe in, which isn't true. The opposite is what really happens, as we can observe. Even though breathing in and out alternates, the last thing we do before death is exhale, so the first act must have been to inhale.

Also, those who explain breathing like this don't say why animals have this function. They make it sound like breathing just happens as part of being alive, but it clearly has control over life and death. When an animal can't breathe, it dies. It's also strange to suggest that the hot air leaving the body is easy to notice, but we can't detect the air entering the lungs and heating up again. It's even more ridiculous to think that breathing involves taking in heat when the opposite is true: we breathe out hot air and take in cool air. When it's hot, we pant because the air coming in isn't cooling us enough, so we have to breathe more frequently.

But we shouldn't think that breathing is for feeding the body like food. Breathing isn't about adding fuel to the body's internal fire, as some have said, with the air acting like food for the flame and then being breathed out. I'll repeat the argument I used earlier against this idea. If that were true, we would see the same thing happening in other animals since they all have body heat. Also, how could breathing create heat? We see that heat comes from food, not air. This theory would also mean that the same passage in the body would be used for taking in food and pushing out waste, but we don't see that happening in other cases.

Empedocles also explained breathing, but he didn't make clear what its purpose is or whether it's universal in all animals. He talked about breathing through the nostrils as if it were the main kind of breathing. But the air that enters through the nostrils also passes through the windpipe and out of the chest, and without the windpipe, the nostrils can't function. Also, if an animal can't breathe through its nose, it's fine. But if it can't breathe through its windpipe, it dies. Nature uses nose breathing for smelling in some animals. The reason why only some animals have it is that, while most animals can smell, they don't all have the same organs for it.

Empedocles also described how breathing works by saying that certain blood vessels hold blood but are not filled with it. These vessels have openings that connect to the air outside the body. The openings are small enough to keep the solid parts of the blood in but large enough for air to pass through. He said that when the blood moves down, air comes in, and this causes inhaling. When the blood moves up, air is pushed out, causing exhaling. He compared this to a water clock, a device used to measure time with water.

Here's how he explained it:

"All things breathe in and out. Their bodies have small tubes that reach the outer edges. These tubes have many channels leading through the nostrils. When the blood moves away, air rushes in. But when the blood moves up, air flows out. This is like a water clock. When a girl puts her hand over the tube and dips it in water, no water enters because the air is trapped. But when she lets the air escape, water rushes in. Just like the water clock, the blood moves, creating space for the air to flow in or out."

That's how he explained breathing. But as we've said, all animals that breathe do so through their windpipe, whether they breathe through their mouth or nose. If he's talking about this kind of breathing, we need to ask how it matches his explanation. The facts seem to go against it. The chest rises like a bellows when we inhale. It makes sense that heat would lift it up and that the blood would gather in the warm area. But the chest sinks back down when we exhale, just like a bellows. The difference is that in breathing, the air comes in and goes out through the same passage, while in a bellows, the air enters and exits through different places.

If Empedocles is only talking about breathing through the nose, he's mistaken. Nose breathing doesn't just involve the nostrils; it also passes through the area near the uvula, at the roof of the mouth. Some of the air goes through the nostrils, and some goes through the mouth, both when we breathe in and when we breathe out.

These are the problems with how other philosophers have explained breathing.

• • •

On Longevity and Shortness of Life

Aristotle's Study of the Secrets of a Long Life

A Modern Translation

Adapted for the Contemporary Reader

Aristotle

Translated by Tim Zengerink

Introduction

Ancient Greece was a civilization famous for its great contributions to philosophy, politics, art, and science. It thrived from the 8th century BCE until the Roman Empire started to decline. Greece's city-states, especially Athens, were the heart of culture and intellectual thought. This was the time when democracy began, impressive buildings like the Parthenon were built, and famous playwrights like Sophocles and Euripides produced their works. The Greeks' curiosity about the world around them laid the foundation for Western philosophy. Thinkers like Socrates, Plato, and later Aristotle, pushed the limits of what people understood about the world.

Greek society was deeply connected to theism, which focused on a large group of gods and goddesses who were believed to control every part of life. But this system did not prevent people from exploring new ideas. In fact, it coexisted with a growing interest in finding logical explanations for nature and human

life. Intellectuals would often debate and discuss these ideas in public places like the Agora. Aristotle grew up in this dynamic environment, learning from earlier philosophers, and later challenging and expanding their ideas.

Aristotle's Life

Aristotle was born in 384 BCE in a small town called Stagira, located in northern Greece. His father, Nicomachus, was a doctor for King Amyntas of Macedon, and this allowed Aristotle to be around the Macedonian royal court from a young age. When his parents passed away, Aristotle was sent to Athens at the age of 17 to pursue his education. Athens was the center of intellectual life in Greece, and Aristotle joined Plato's Academy, which was the most respected school of the time. The Academy was a place where students discussed everything from ethics to science. Although Aristotle learned a lot from Plato, he did not always agree with him, especially when it came to metaphysics, which deals with the nature of reality.

After spending almost 20 years at the Academy, Aristotle left Athens around 347 BCE after Plato's death. He traveled around different cities in Greece, continuing to study and learn. In 343 BCE, he was

invited to the court of King Philip II of Macedon, where he became the tutor of Philip's son, Alexander, who would later become known as Alexander the Great. Aristotle taught Alexander about philosophy, ethics, politics, and science. Aristotle's influence is visible in Alexander's leadership style, which showed respect for knowledge and strategic thinking.

After teaching Alexander, Aristotle returned to Athens in 335 BCE, where he opened his own school called the Lyceum. Unlike Plato's Academy, the Lyceum focused more on recording knowledge and observing nature. Aristotle and his students performed research, studied animals, and took notes on what they observed. The Lyceum became a major center of learning, and it rivaled Plato's Academy. This is also where Aristotle wrote many of his famous works.

Later in life, after the death of Alexander in 323 BCE, the political climate in Athens became difficult for Aristotle because of his connections to the Macedonian court. Accused of disrespecting the gods, Aristotle decided to leave Athens. He fled to Chalcis, where he passed away in 322 BCE. Even though he had to leave Athens, his legacy lived on through his many writings and the influence of his school, the Lyceum.

Aristotle's Impact on Western Thought

No figure looms larger over the development of Western philosophy and science than Aristotle. A student of Plato and tutor to Alexander the Great, he unified logic, ethics, politics, rhetoric, and metaphysics into a coherent system that shaped intellectual inquiry for centuries. Although his writings reflect the best knowledge of his era, they also reveal a distinctive way of understanding the world—one that balances observation with rigorous logical analysis. Over time, this method has profoundly influenced everything from political theory to modern scientific methodology.

Aristotle approached knowledge as an interconnected whole, seeing each field of study as a vital path toward truth. While many earlier thinkers focused on abstract concepts, he emphasized direct observation of the natural world. By systematically examining and classifying what he saw, Aristotle laid the groundwork for the empirical methods now central to modern science. Although our understanding of nature has evolved, his legacy endures in today's emphasis on evidence-based research.

Logic: The Foundation of Rational Inquiry

Often hailed as the "father of formal logic," Aristotle introduced a system of reasoning that shaped intellectual discourse for over two millennia. In works like the Organon, he analyzed how valid conclusions are drawn from premises and introduced syllogisms—deductive arguments that became standard tools in philosophy, theology, and science. Even contemporary logic, despite its modern mathematical and symbolic advancements, can trace many of its core principles back to Aristotle's pioneering analyses.

Metaphysics: Exploring the Nature of Reality

Aristotle's Metaphysics offered one of the earliest comprehensive explorations of existence at its most fundamental level. There, he described the nature of "being qua being" and introduced the concepts of potentiality and actuality to explain how things change and develop. These ideas deeply influenced medieval scholastics—both Christian and Islamic—who integrated Aristotelian reasoning into their theological frameworks. Today, discussions about consciousness, identity, and free will still reference these Aristotelian notions.

Ethics and the Pursuit of the Good Life

In the Nicomachean Ethics, Aristotle proposed that the ultimate aim of human life is eudaimonia, often translated as "happiness" or "flourishing." He argued that we achieve this through virtue, developed by cultivating good habits guided by reason. His famous Doctrine of the Mean asserts that moral virtue resides between two extremes—for instance, courage lies between recklessness and cowardice. This focus on character formation has profoundly shaped the tradition known as "virtue ethics," influencing modern debates on moral education, personal development, and what it means to live well.

Politics: The Role of the Individual in the City-State

Aristotle's practical approach to ethics naturally extended into political theory. In Politics, he explored various forms of government—monarchy, aristocracy, oligarchy, democracy—and weighed their merits and pitfalls. For Aristotle, a well-ordered polis (city-state) exists not merely for survival or trade but to enable its citizens to live virtuous, fulfilling lives. His conviction that ethics

and politics are intertwined remains influential, informing contemporary discussions on citizenship, governance, and justice.

Rhetoric: The Art of Persuasion

In his treatise Rhetoric, Aristotle examined how persuasion works, detailing how arguments must appeal to ethos (credibility), pathos (emotion), and logos (logic). This clear framework for effective communication continues to guide public speakers, legal advocates, and writers. From ancient courtroom orations to modern political campaigns, Aristotelian rhetoric underpins many of the strategies people use to sway audiences and shape public opinion.

Beyond these core subjects, Aristotle made significant contributions to biology, physics, psychology, and aesthetics. In the Poetics, for example, he investigated why humans respond so powerfully to tragic drama, pioneering the concept of catharsis—the emotional release that audiences feel through art. Throughout the medieval period, thinkers like Thomas Aquinas integrated Aristotle's theories into Christian theology, while Islamic philosophers such as Avicenna and Averroes preserved, interpreted, and expanded upon his works.

Across centuries of reinterpretation and debate, Aristotle remains a living voice in contemporary thought. His insistence on systematically gathering evidence and connecting it to logical principles laid the foundation for what we now recognize as the scientific method. His inquiries into human flourishing, civic responsibility, and the nature of argument continue to spark discussion and inspire new research. From personal ethics to societal organization, Aristotle's ideas help us frame enduring questions about how best to live, learn, and understand reality.

In sum, Aristotle stands as a foundational pillar of Western thought. He bridged abstract theorizing and practical inquiry, bequeathing a vision of knowledge that values both reason and experience. From ethics and politics to science and art, his ideas have been woven into countless intellectual traditions. Even today, as we grapple with questions of morality, governance, and truth, we walk in the footsteps of an ancient thinker whose breadth of insight and depth of analysis continue to guide our pursuit of wisdom.

Final Thoughts

By preserving Aristotle's legacy, we protect the intellectual depth and rigor that defined his way

of understanding the world. His systematic way of asking questions, his classification of knowledge, and his ethical theories are still relevant today, providing a model for critical thinking across many subjects. This preservation is important not just for philosophy students but for anyone interested in the foundations of human thought and the development of ideas that shape the world we live in.

One of the difficulties in studying Aristotle's work is that his ideas and language are complex. Translating these works into our modern language is a key step in making his profound insights easier for more people to understand. By putting his ideas into today's language, more readers can engage with his thoughts, even if they don't have a background in classical studies. Making Aristotle's work accessible means adapting them to modern ways of thinking without losing their original depth. This helps bridge the gap between ancient and modern readers, making sure Aristotle's work stays relevant.

On Longevity and Shortness of Life

We need to investigate why some animals live long lives while others have short ones, and what causes the length or shortness of life.

To start, we need to ask whether animals and plants all have the same reason for living longer or shorter lives, or if the reasons are different. Some plants also live a long time, while others only last for a year.

Also, we should ask whether a long life and being healthy always go together, or if it's possible to live a short life but still be healthy. In some cases, disease and a short life may go hand in hand, but in others, poor health might not prevent a long life.

We've already talked about sleep and waking, and later we'll talk about life and death, and health and disease, where it makes sense to do so in the study of nature. For now, we're focusing on why some creatures live longer and others live shorter lives. This difference shows up not only between whole groups of animals, but also between individuals of the same species. For example, humans live longer than horses, but even among humans, some live longer than others. The place where people live also matters—people in warm climates tend to live longer, while those in cold climates often live shorter lives. There are also differences between individuals living in the same area.

To figure this out, we need to first answer the question: What makes some natural things easy to destroy and others not? Fire and water, and things related to them, don't have the same effects—they cause both the creation and destruction of things. So, it makes sense that everything made from fire and water would share these qualities, as long as they aren't just simple combinations of things like a house.

In other cases, the way things break down is unique to them. For example, knowledge, health, and disease disappear even though the thing they're found in (like the body or the mind) isn't destroyed. For instance, ignorance is replaced by learning or remembering, while knowledge turns into forgetfulness or error. But when a living thing dies, the health or knowledge it had also disappears. This can help us think about the soul, too. If the soul's connection to the body were like knowledge's connection to the mind, then it would have a different way of breaking down. But since the soul doesn't have this kind of connection, its relationship with the body must be different.

Some people might ask if there's a place where things that usually die, like fire, can't be destroyed, like in the upper regions of the sky where there's no opposite force. Opposites destroy each other, and through this destruction, the things connected to them are also destroyed. But if something has no opposite, or is in a place where its opposite can't reach it, it can't be destroyed. However, this isn't always true, because anything that contains matter will have some kind of opposite. For example, heat and straightness can be present in every part of something, but nothing can be only hot or straight. If that were possible, then qualities like heat or straightness would exist on their own, which they don't. And when something has both active and passive qualities, one will always affect the other, causing change. Waste, which is left over from these changes, can also act as an opposite and cause destruction.

A smaller flame can be burned up by a larger one because the smaller one uses up its fuel slowly, while the bigger one burns it up quickly.

This means that all things are constantly changing, being created, and being destroyed. Their environment can help or harm them, making them last longer or shorter than they naturally would. But nothing can live forever when it has opposite qualities, because these opposites cause things to change their location, size, or qualities over time.

We can see that neither the biggest animals nor the smallest ones are the most resistant to decay. For example, horses live shorter lives than humans, and many insects only live for a year. The same goes for plants—some only last a year. Bloodless animals don't live the longest either. For example, bees live longer than some animals with blood, even though they don't have any. And animals that live on land don't live longer than sea creatures. Crabs and mollusks, for example, don't live long lives, despite living in the sea.

Generally, the longest-lived things are plants, like the date palm. Next come animals with blood, especially those with legs. For example, humans and elephants are among the longest-lived animals. Usually, bigger animals live longer than smaller ones, as most long-lived animals are also large, like the ones I just mentioned.

Now, let's look at the reasons behind these facts. Animals are naturally warm and moist, and staying alive depends on keeping this balance. Old age, however, is dry and cold, like a dead body. You can see this with your own eyes. The bodies of all living things are made of four basic elements: hot, cold, dry, and moist. So, as things age, they must become dry. This explains why fat things don't decay as easily. Fat contains air, which is like fire, and fire doesn't break down easily.

Also, animals need a lot of moisture to stay alive. A small amount of moisture dries up quickly, which is why both large plants and animals usually live longer than smaller ones, as I mentioned earlier. It's not just the amount of moisture that matters, though. The quality of the moisture is also important. It must be both plentiful and warm so that it doesn't freeze or dry up too easily.

This is why humans live longer than some larger animals. Even though humans may have less moisture, the quality of their moisture makes up for the smaller amount.

In some animals, fat helps prevent drying out and freezing, while in others, the moisture has a different quality. Also, things that don't produce much waste live longer. Waste can cause disease or death because it weakens the body. Animals that produce a lot of waste or seed tend to age quickly. Seed is a type of residue, and losing it makes the body drier. This is why mules live longer than horses or donkeys, and why females often live longer than males, especially in species where males are very sexual. For example, male sparrows have shorter lives than females. Males who do a lot of hard work also live shorter lives because hard work causes dryness, and old age is dry. But generally, males live longer than females because males have more natural warmth.

Animals in warm climates also live longer than those in cold climates for the same reason. Warmth helps them grow larger and live longer. In cold places, the moisture in animals is more watery and freezes easily, which prevents growth. This is why cold-blooded animals like snakes and lizards grow larger in warm places. Even sea creatures like shellfish grow larger in the warm waters of the Red Sea. Warm moisture in these areas helps them both grow and live longer. But in cold areas, animals are smaller and have shorter lives because the cold freezes their moisture.

Both plants and animals will die if they aren't fed, because they will use up their own body's resources. It's like a small flame being burned up by a larger one that uses all the fuel. The natural warmth in an animal's body, which helps with digestion, will consume the materials in the body if there's no food to replace it.

Sea creatures live shorter lives than land animals, not just because they are moist, but because their moisture is watery, which is cold and easily frozen. For the same reason, bloodless animals die easily unless they are large. They don't have fat or sweetness in their bodies. Fat is sweet in animals, which is why bees live longer than some larger animals.

Plants tend to live longer than animals. This is because they have less water, so they don't freeze as easily. Also, plants have a certain oiliness and thickness that helps them hold onto moisture without drying out, even though they are naturally dry and earthy.

We need to understand why trees can last so long, as this is unique to them and not seen in animals, except in some insects.

Plants constantly renew themselves, which is why they can live for a long time. New shoots keep growing while the older parts age. The same thing happens with the roots. But these changes don't happen at the same time. First, the trunk and branches die, and new ones grow beside them. Then, when that happens, new roots grow from the surviving part of the plant. This cycle continues—one part dies while another grows—allowing the plant to live a long life.

There's a similarity between plants and insects, as mentioned before. Both can continue living even after being divided, and one can become two or more. However, insects, though they can survive after being divided, don't live for long because they don't have the organs needed to sustain life, and the separated parts can't develop new organs. In plants, each part has the potential to grow both roots and a stem. This allows plants to keep growing, with one part renewing while another part grows old, giving them a longer life. A similar process happens when you take a cutting from a plant. The cutting is part of the plant, and it can continue to live and grow even though it's no longer attached. In the case of plants, this ongoing renewal is what keeps them alive for so long. The reason for this is that the life force of the plant is present in every part of it.

The same kind of things happen in both plants and animals. In animals, males generally live longer. Males have larger upper bodies compared to their lower bodies (making them more compact or stocky than females), and the upper body is where warmth is found, while the lower body is cooler. In plants, those that have large root systems, like trees, also live longer. In plants, the roots are like the head or the upper part, and annual plants, which only live for a year, grow more in their lower parts and produce fruit.

We'll look at these things more deeply when we discuss plants specifically. But this explains why some animals live longer lives and others have shorter ones. Next, we'll explore youth, old age, life, and death. Understanding these topics will complete our study of animals.

• • •

live longest. In plants, the roots are like the head or the upper part, and annual plants, which only live for a year, grow more in their lower parts and produce fruit.

We'll look at these things more deeply when we discuss plants specifically. But this explains why some animals live longer and others have shorter ones. Last, we'll explore youth, old age, life, and death. Understanding these topics will complete our study of animals.

On Breathing

Understanding the Connection Between Breath and Life

A Modern Translation

Adapted for the Contemporary Reader

Aristotle

Translated by Tim Zengerink

Introduction

Ancient Greece was a civilization famous for its great contributions to philosophy, politics, art, and science. It thrived from the 8th century BCE until the Roman Empire started to decline. Greece's city-states, especially Athens, were the heart of culture and intellectual thought. This was the time when democracy began, impressive buildings like the Parthenon were built, and famous playwrights like Sophocles and Euripides produced their works. The Greeks' curiosity about the world around them laid the foundation for Western philosophy. Thinkers like Socrates, Plato, and later Aristotle, pushed the limits of what people understood about the world.

Greek society was deeply connected to theism, which focused on a large group of gods and goddesses who were believed to control every part of life. But this system did not prevent people from exploring new ideas. In fact, it coexisted with a growing interest in finding logical explanations for nature and human

life. Intellectuals would often debate and discuss these ideas in public places like the Agora. Aristotle grew up in this dynamic environment, learning from earlier philosophers, and later challenging and expanding their ideas.

Aristotle's Life

Aristotle was born in 384 BCE in a small town called Stagira, located in northern Greece. His father, Nicomachus, was a doctor for King Amyntas of Macedon, and this allowed Aristotle to be around the Macedonian royal court from a young age. When his parents passed away, Aristotle was sent to Athens at the age of 17 to pursue his education. Athens was the center of intellectual life in Greece, and Aristotle joined Plato's Academy, which was the most respected school of the time. The Academy was a place where students discussed everything from ethics to science. Although Aristotle learned a lot from Plato, he did not always agree with him, especially when it came to metaphysics, which deals with the nature of reality.

After spending almost 20 years at the Academy, Aristotle left Athens around 347 BCE after Plato's death. He traveled around different cities in Greece, continuing to study and learn. In 343 BCE, he was

invited to the court of King Philip II of Macedon, where he became the tutor of Philip's son, Alexander, who would later become known as Alexander the Great. Aristotle taught Alexander about philosophy, ethics, politics, and science. Aristotle's influence is visible in Alexander's leadership style, which showed respect for knowledge and strategic thinking.

After teaching Alexander, Aristotle returned to Athens in 335 BCE, where he opened his own school called the Lyceum. Unlike Plato's Academy, the Lyceum focused more on recording knowledge and observing nature. Aristotle and his students performed research, studied animals, and took notes on what they observed. The Lyceum became a major center of learning, and it rivaled Plato's Academy. This is also where Aristotle wrote many of his famous works.

Later in life, after the death of Alexander in 323 BCE, the political climate in Athens became difficult for Aristotle because of his connections to the Macedonian court. Accused of disrespecting the gods, Aristotle decided to leave Athens. He fled to Chalcis, where he passed away in 322 BCE. Even though he had to leave Athens, his legacy lived on through his many writings and the influence of his school, the Lyceum.

Aristotle's Impact on Western Thought

No figure looms larger over the development of Western philosophy and science than Aristotle. A student of Plato and tutor to Alexander the Great, he unified logic, ethics, politics, rhetoric, and metaphysics into a coherent system that shaped intellectual inquiry for centuries. Although his writings reflect the best knowledge of his era, they also reveal a distinctive way of understanding the world—one that balances observation with rigorous logical analysis. Over time, this method has profoundly influenced everything from political theory to modern scientific methodology.

Aristotle approached knowledge as an interconnected whole, seeing each field of study as a vital path toward truth. While many earlier thinkers focused on abstract concepts, he emphasized direct observation of the natural world. By systematically examining and classifying what he saw, Aristotle laid the groundwork for the empirical methods now central to modern science. Although our understanding of nature has evolved, his legacy endures in today's emphasis on evidence-based research.

Logic: The Foundation of Rational Inquiry

Often hailed as the "father of formal logic," Aristotle introduced a system of reasoning that shaped intellectual discourse for over two millennia. In works like the Organon, he analyzed how valid conclusions are drawn from premises and introduced syllogisms—deductive arguments that became standard tools in philosophy, theology, and science. Even contemporary logic, despite its modern mathematical and symbolic advancements, can trace many of its core principles back to Aristotle's pioneering analyses.

Metaphysics: Exploring the Nature of Reality

Aristotle's Metaphysics offered one of the earliest comprehensive explorations of existence at its most fundamental level. There, he described the nature of "being qua being" and introduced the concepts of potentiality and actuality to explain how things change and develop. These ideas deeply influenced medieval scholastics—both Christian and Islamic—who integrated Aristotelian reasoning into their theological frameworks. Today, discussions about consciousness, identity, and free will still reference these Aristotelian notions.

Ethics and the Pursuit of the Good Life

In the Nicomachean Ethics, Aristotle proposed that the ultimate aim of human life is eudaimonia, often translated as "happiness" or "flourishing." He argued that we achieve this through virtue, developed by cultivating good habits guided by reason. His famous Doctrine of the Mean asserts that moral virtue resides between two extremes—for instance, courage lies between recklessness and cowardice. This focus on character formation has profoundly shaped the tradition known as "virtue ethics," influencing modern debates on moral education, personal development, and what it means to live well.

Politics: The Role of the Individual in the City-State

Aristotle's practical approach to ethics naturally extended into political theory. In Politics, he explored various forms of government—monarchy, aristocracy, oligarchy, democracy—and weighed their merits and pitfalls. For Aristotle, a well-ordered polis (city-state) exists not merely for survival or trade but to enable its citizens to live virtuous, fulfilling lives. His conviction that ethics

and politics are intertwined remains influential, informing contemporary discussions on citizenship, governance, and justice.

Rhetoric: The Art of Persuasion

In his treatise Rhetoric, Aristotle examined how persuasion works, detailing how arguments must appeal to ethos (credibility), pathos (emotion), and logos (logic). This clear framework for effective communication continues to guide public speakers, legal advocates, and writers. From ancient courtroom orations to modern political campaigns, Aristotelian rhetoric underpins many of the strategies people use to sway audiences and shape public opinion.

Beyond these core subjects, Aristotle made significant contributions to biology, physics, psychology, and aesthetics. In the Poetics, for example, he investigated why humans respond so powerfully to tragic drama, pioneering the concept of catharsis—the emotional release that audiences feel through art. Throughout the medieval period, thinkers like Thomas Aquinas integrated Aristotle's theories into Christian theology, while Islamic philosophers such as Avicenna and Averroes preserved, interpreted, and expanded upon his works.

Across centuries of reinterpretation and debate, Aristotle remains a living voice in contemporary thought. His insistence on systematically gathering evidence and connecting it to logical principles laid the foundation for what we now recognize as the scientific method. His inquiries into human flourishing, civic responsibility, and the nature of argument continue to spark discussion and inspire new research. From personal ethics to societal organization, Aristotle's ideas help us frame enduring questions about how best to live, learn, and understand reality.

In sum, Aristotle stands as a foundational pillar of Western thought. He bridged abstract theorizing and practical inquiry, bequeathing a vision of knowledge that values both reason and experience. From ethics and politics to science and art, his ideas have been woven into countless intellectual traditions. Even today, as we grapple with questions of morality, governance, and truth, we walk in the footsteps of an ancient thinker whose breadth of insight and depth of analysis continue to guide our pursuit of wisdom.

Final Thoughts

By preserving Aristotle's legacy, we protect the intellectual depth and rigor that defined his way

of understanding the world. His systematic way of asking questions, his classification of knowledge, and his ethical theories are still relevant today, providing a model for critical thinking across many subjects. This preservation is important not just for philosophy students but for anyone interested in the foundations of human thought and the development of ideas that shape the world we live in.

One of the difficulties in studying Aristotle's work is that his ideas and language are complex. Translating these works into our modern language is a key step in making his profound insights easier for more people to understand. By putting his ideas into today's language, more readers can engage with his thoughts, even if they don't have a background in classical studies. Making Aristotle's work accessible means adapting them to modern ways of thinking without losing their original depth. This helps bridge the gap between ancient and modern readers, making sure Aristotle's work stays relevant.

Section 1

We have already mentioned that life and the presence of a soul involve a certain warmth. Even the process of digesting food, which provides nutrition for animals, doesn't happen without the soul and warmth, because in all cases, digestion is due to heat. That's why the main part of the soul responsible for nutrition must be located in the part of the body where this principle is active. This part is between where food enters and where waste is expelled. In animals without blood, this part doesn't have a name, but in animals with blood, it's called the heart. The blood provides the nourishment from which the animal's organs are made. So, the blood vessels must have the same starting point since they exist to support the blood by serving as its containers. In animals with blood, the heart is where the veins start; they don't pass through it, but instead, they spread out from it, as we can see when we study dissections.

Other abilities of the soul can't exist without the power of nutrition (as explained in the treatise *On the Soul*), and this power depends on natural heat, which Nature has activated by bringing it to life. But fire, as we have already said, can be destroyed in two ways—by going out or burning out. It can be put out by its opposite forces. So, fire can be extinguished by surrounding cold, whether it's in large amounts or spread out (though it happens faster when spread out). This kind of destruction happens by force both in living and non-living things, for cutting an animal apart or freezing it with extreme cold causes death. However, burning out happens when there is too much heat; if the heat is too intense and nothing adds new fuel, the fire will go out because it burns out, not because of cold. So, if it's going to keep going, it needs to be cooled down because cold prevents this kind of burnout.

Some animals live in water, while others live on land. For very small, bloodless animals, the cooling effect of the surrounding water or air is enough to prevent them from burning out due to heat. Since they don't have much heat, they don't need much cold to keep them balanced. This also explains why these animals don't live long, because being small means they have less ability to resist extremes. But some insects live longer, even though they are bloodless like the others, and they have a deep indentation below their middle section to allow cooling through a thinner membrane. These insects are warmer and need more cooling, like bees (some of which live for seven years) and all insects that make a humming noise, such as wasps, beetles, and crickets. They make a sound that's like panting by using air, as the air inside them causes a rising and falling movement that creates friction against the membrane. The way they move this area is similar to how the lungs move in animals that breathe, or how gills move in fish. What happens is like when an animal that breathes air is suffocated by blocking its mouth, causing the lungs to make a similar rising and falling movement. In these animals, this internal movement isn't enough for cooling, but in insects, it is. By creating friction against the membrane, they make the humming sound, as we said, similar to how children make sounds by blowing through a reed covered by a thin membrane. This is also how crickets make their songs; they have more heat and a deeper indentation at the waist, while those that don't make noise have no such indentation.

Animals that have blood and lungs, but whose lungs have little blood and are spongy, can sometimes live for a long time without breathing, because the lung, with its small amount of blood or liquid, can rise very high, and its own movement can keep cooling the body for a long time. But eventually, this is not enough, and the animal dies from suffocation if it doesn't breathe, as we've already mentioned. Exhaustion due to a lack of cooling is called suffocation, and anything that dies this way is said to be suffocated.

We've already said that insects don't breathe like other animals, and we can observe this in small creatures like flies and bees, which can move around in a liquid for a long time as long as it's not too hot or cold. However, animals with little strength tend to breathe more often. These animals die from what we call suffocation when their stomach fills up and the heat in their middle part is lost. This is also why they can revive after being in ashes for some time.

Among water animals, those without blood can live longer in air than those with blood, like fish. Since they have a small amount of heat, the air can cool them for a long time, as we see in animals like crabs and octopuses. However, the air is not enough to keep them alive because they don't have enough heat. Many fish can also live in the soil, though they stay still, and they can be found by digging. All animals that don't have lungs or have bloodless lungs need less cooling.

Regarding bloodless animals, we've explained that some rely on the surrounding air and others on fluids to maintain life. But for animals with blood and a heart, all those with lungs take in air and cool themselves by breathing in and out. All animals that give birth to live young and do so inside their bodies (unlike the Selachia, which give birth outside) have lungs, as do oviparous animals, such as birds and scaly animals like tortoises, lizards, and snakes. In the first group, the lungs are filled with blood, but in most of the latter, the lungs are spongy. So, they breathe less often, as we've said before. This function is also found in animals that live in water, like water snakes, frogs, crocodiles, and turtles, whether they live in the sea or on land, as well as in seals.

All these animals give birth on land and sleep on land, or when they sleep in water, they keep their heads above the surface to breathe. But animals with gills cool themselves by taking in water; this includes Selachia and other animals without legs. Fish have no legs, and their fins are named for their resemblance to wings. However, one animal with legs, the tadpole, has gills.

No animal has both lungs and gills, and the reason is that lungs are made for cooling through air (their name, "pneumon," seems to come from their function as a container for breath), while gills are for cooling through water. Since one tool is enough for one purpose, Nature doesn't make unnecessary organs. So, some animals have gills, others have lungs, but none have both.

Every animal needs food to live and cooling to prevent death. Nature uses the same organ for both tasks. For example, in some animals, the tongue is used both to taste food and for speaking. In animals with lungs, the mouth is used to break down food and to let air in and out. In animals without lungs or that don't breathe, the mouth is just used to break down food, while in animals that need cooling, gills are made for this purpose.

We'll explain later how these organs produce cooling. But to make sure food doesn't interfere with breathing, both respiring animals and those that take in water have a similar system. When they breathe, they don't take in food, because food, whether liquid or dry, could get into the windpipe and cause suffocation by blocking the lungs. The windpipe is located in front of the esophagus, through which food goes into the stomach. In blooded quadrupeds, there is a lid called the epiglottis over the windpipe. In birds and egg-laying quadrupeds, this covering is missing, but they close their windpipes by contracting them. When swallowing food, birds contract the windpipe while mammals close the epiglottis. Once the food has passed, the epiglottis is raised, or the windpipe expands, allowing air to enter and cool the body. In animals with gills, water is expelled first, then food enters the mouth. They don't have a windpipe, so they aren't harmed by liquids entering their windpipe, only by liquids entering the stomach. This is why these animals quickly expel water and grab their food. Their teeth are sharp and often arranged like a saw because they can't chew their food.

Among water animals, cetaceans, like dolphins and whales, may seem puzzling, but they can be explained. Examples of these animals include dolphins, whales, and others with blowholes. They don't have legs but do have lungs, even though they live in water. They have lungs for cooling, as we mentioned, but they don't take in water to cool themselves. Instead, they cool down by breathing because they have lungs. That's why they sleep with their heads out of the water, and dolphins even snore. If they get caught in nets, they die quickly from suffocation because they can't breathe. So, they can be seen coming to the surface to breathe. Since they need to eat in the water, they take in water and expel it through their blowholes, just as fish expel water through their gills. The blowhole is placed in front of the brain, where it releases the water without touching any of the blood-filled organs.

Mollusks and crustaceans, like crabs, also take in water for the same reason. These animals don't need cooling because they don't have much heat and are bloodless. The surrounding water cools them enough. But when they eat, they take in water, and they have to expel it to avoid swallowing it along with the food. Crustaceans, like crabs and lobsters, expel water through the folds beside their hairy parts, while cuttlefish and octopuses use the hollow above their heads. There's a more detailed explanation of these animals in *The History of Animals*.

This explains why animals take in water for cooling and how those that live in water must eat in it as well.

We must now explain how cooling happens in animals that breathe and those with gills. We've already said that all animals with lungs breathe. The reason some creatures have lungs, and those that do need to breathe, is that higher animals have more heat. Since they have a higher soul and nature than plants, they need this. Animals with more blood and warmth in their lungs tend to be larger, and the animal with the purest and most abundant blood in the lungs is the most upright—this is man. The reason man alone stands with his upper part directed toward the upper part of the universe is that he has such lungs.

So, the lungs must be considered an essential part of the animal's nature, both in humans and in other animals.

This is the purpose of cooling. As for the cause behind this, we must believe that nature made animals this way, just as it made many other animals with different compositions. Some animals have more earth in their makeup, like plants, while others, like aquatic animals, have more water. Winged and land animals have more air and fire, respectively. Each thing exists in the region that suits the element most abundant in its composition.

Empedocles was wrong when he said that animals with the most warmth and fire live in water to balance the heat in their bodies. He thought that since they lack cold and fluid, living in water keeps them alive, as water has less heat than air. But it makes no sense that water animals would all originate on land and then move to the water, especially since most of them have no legs. Yet, he said that they were first created on land and then moved to the water. But it's clear that water animals aren't warmer than land animals, as some have no blood at all, and others have very little.

We've already discussed what kinds of animals should be considered warm and what kinds cold. While

Empedocles' idea has some logic, his explanation is wrong. A condition that is too extreme is balanced by its opposite, but the best way for an animal's body to stay healthy is to be in an environment similar to its own nature. There's a difference between what an animal is made of and the condition of that material. For example, if nature made something out of wax or ice, it wouldn't be kept safe in a hot place because heat would quickly destroy it, as heat melts what cold freezes. Likewise, something made of salt or nitre wouldn't be placed in water because water would dissolve it, as its structure depends on being dry and warm.

So, if all bodies are made of wet and dry materials, it makes sense that things made mostly of wet and cold elements would live in liquid environments. And if they are cold, they would exist in cold places, while things made mostly of dry elements would be found on land. Trees, for instance, don't grow in water but on dry land. But according to Empedocles' theory, they should live in water because they are so dry, just like things that are very fiery. They would move to water, not because of the cold, but because of its fluid nature.

In reality, the natural state of materials is suited to the regions they exist in. Liquids belong in liquid environments, dry things on land, and warm things in the air. However, in terms of a body's condition, a cold environment helps balance out too much heat, while a warm one helps balance too much cold. The region around the animal adjusts the excess condition in its body. The regions where things live and the changing seasons also help fix such imbalances. But while a body's condition can be the opposite of its surroundings, the material that makes up the body cannot be. This explains why some animals are aquatic and others are terrestrial, and why some have lungs while others do not. It's not because of the amount of heat in their bodies, as Empedocles claimed.

The reason animals with lungs, especially those with lungs full of blood, breathe air is because the lungs are spongy and full of tubes. The lungs also have more blood than any other organ. All animals with blood-filled lungs need to cool down quickly because they don't have much room for changes in their body heat. The air needs to get through the entire lung because of the large amount of blood and heat it holds. Air can easily do this because it's light and can spread everywhere quickly, allowing it to cool down the body. Water, on the other hand, can't do this as easily.

This explains why animals with blood-filled lungs breathe more often—the more heat they have, the more cooling they need. Also, air can easily reach the source of heat in the heart.

To understand how the heart connects to the lungs through passages, we should look at dissections and the information in the *History of Animals*. The main reason animals need cooling is that the soul and fire come together in the heart. Breathing is how animals with lungs and a heart cool themselves. But for animals like fish, which live in water and don't have lungs, cooling happens through the gills using water. If you want to see how the heart connects to the gills, you need to look at dissections, and for more details, refer to *Natural History*. For now, we can sum it up like this.

It might seem like the heart is in a different position in land animals and fish, but the position is actually the same. The tip of the heart points in the direction the animal tilts its head. In fish, the tip of the heart points toward the mouth, since they don't tilt their heads the same way land animals do. From the tip of the heart, a large, strong tube runs to the center where all the gills meet. This is the biggest tube, but there are others on either side of the heart that go to each gill. Water constantly flows through the gills, cooling the heart.

In the same way fish move their gills, animals that breathe raise and lower their chest as they inhale and exhale. If there isn't enough fresh air, or if the air isn't replaced, they suffocate because the air, after touching the blood, heats up quickly. The heat from the blood cancels out the cooling effect, and when animals can't move their lungs (or fish can't move their gills) due to sickness or old age, they die.

Being born and dying are common to all animals, but there are different ways these things happen. There are different types of death, though they all have something in common. There is violent death, caused by something outside the body, and natural death, caused by something inside the body, built into the way the body is made. It's not something that comes from outside. For plants, this is called withering; for animals, it's called aging. Death and decay happen to everything that is fully developed, though it can also happen to things that aren't fully developed, like eggs or seeds before they sprout roots.

Death always happens due to a loss of heat, and in fully developed creatures, this happens when heat runs out in the organ that is the source of the creature's essential life. As we've said, this organ is located between the upper and lower parts of the body. In plants, it's between the root and the stem, and in animals with blood, it's the heart. In bloodless animals, it's the equivalent part of their body. Some animals have many potential sources of life, though they actually have only one. This explains why some insects can keep living even when they are cut in half, and why even some animals with blood can live for a long time after their heart is removed. For example, tortoises can still move their legs as long as they have their shell, which is due to their naturally weaker constitution, as we see in insects too.

Life ends when the heat that sustains it is no longer cooled properly. As I've said before, the heat burns itself up. So, when the lungs in one type of animal, or the gills in another, dry out over time, they become hard and earthy, unable to move. They can't expand or contract anymore. Eventually, the fire goes out due to exhaustion.

This is why even a small disturbance can cause death in old age. There isn't much heat left because most of it has been used up over the long life. Any extra strain on the body can quickly extinguish what's left. It's like the heart contains a small, weak flame that can easily be put out by the slightest movement. This is why death in old age is painless—there's no need for a violent event to cause it, and the soul departs quietly without feeling anything. Diseases that harden the lungs, such as tumors or excess heat from fevers, speed up breathing because the lungs can't move much either up or down. When the lungs can't move at all, breathing stops, and death follows.

Being born is when an animal first shares in the life-giving soul through warmth, and life is the process of keeping this connection. Youth is the time when the organ for cooling grows, old age is when it starts to decay, and the time in between is the prime of life.

A violent death happens when the vital heat is put out or burns out (both can cause death), while natural death happens when the heat runs out over time and life ends. For plants, this is called withering; for animals, it's called dying. In old age, death is caused by the body's inability to keep cooling itself due to the passage of time. This is our explanation of birth, life, and death, and why they happen in animals.

It is clear why animals that breathe air suffocate in water, and why fish suffocate in air. For fish, water provides the cooling they need, while for animals that breathe air, the air does the same. When either is taken away by a change in their environment, the function is lost.

We must also explain why gills and lungs move the way they do, and how this movement allows air or water to come in and go out. Here's how these organs are structured.

There are three things related to the heart that might seem similar but are actually different: palpitation, pulsation, and respiration.

Palpitation happens when the hot substance in the heart rushes together due to the cooling effect of waste products. This happens in conditions like spasms and other illnesses. It also occurs when you're scared, because when you're afraid, the upper parts of your body become cold, and the hot substance retreats to the heart. This causes the heart to palpitate because the heat is squeezed into such a small space that sometimes life is extinguished, and animals can die from fear and the disturbance it causes.

The constant beating of the heart is similar to the throbbing of an abscess. However, an abscess is painful because the blood changes in an unnatural way, and the throbbing continues until the matter inside is discharged. This process is similar to boiling, where heat turns liquid into vapor and expands it. But in an abscess, if nothing evaporates, the liquid thickens, and the process ends in the formation of pus. In boiling, it ends with the liquid escaping from the container.

In the heart, the beating is caused by heat expanding the liquid, which comes from food. This happens when the liquid rises to the outer wall of the heart and continues without stopping. There is always a constant flow of liquid that turns into blood, and the heart is where blood is first formed. We can see this in the early stages of life, as the heart contains blood before the veins become clear. This is why young people have faster pulses than older people, as there's more vapor being produced in the young.

All veins pulse at the same time because they are connected to the heart. Since the heart always beats, the veins also beat continuously and in sync with the heart.

So, palpitation is the heart's reaction to being squeezed by cold, while pulsation is caused by the heated liquid turning into vapor.

Respiration happens when the hot substance, which is the source of nutrition, grows. This part of the body needs more nutrition than other parts because it feeds them. As it grows, it makes the organ expand. This organ is built like a pair of bellows, similar to those used by blacksmiths. The heart and lungs have a similar shape. This structure must be double because the source of nutrition needs to be at the center of the natural forces.

As the organ expands, it causes the surrounding parts to rise. We can see this happen when people breathe. They lift their chest because the part inside the chest expands the same way. When this part expands, air rushes in like it would in bellows. The air is cold, so it cools the heat by reducing the excess fire. When the organ shrinks, the air that entered is pushed back out. When air enters, it's cold, but when it exits, it's warm because it has been in contact with the heat in the organ. This is especially true for animals with lungs full of blood. The lung has many tubes with blood vessels next to them, so it seems like the whole lung is full of blood. The movement of air inward is called respiration, and the movement outward is called expiration. This process continues for as long as the animal lives, as the organ keeps moving constantly. Life is tied to this constant movement of air in and out.

The movement of gills in fish happens in the same way. When the hot substance in the blood rises, the gills rise too and let water pass through. When the heat is cooled and flows back to the heart, the gills contract and push the water out. As the heat in the heart rises and then cools, this process repeats. So, just as breathing is tied to life and death in air-breathing animals, water entering and exiting is tied to life and death in fish.

We have now covered life, death, and related topics. But health and disease also deserve the attention of scientists, not just doctors, when it comes to understanding their causes. It's important to recognize the difference between the work of scientists and that of physicians, although they overlap in some ways. Doctors who are well-educated often mention natural science and claim that their methods come from it. On the other hand, the best scientists often take their studies so far that they end up discussing medical principles too.

• • •

The End

Thank you for Reading

You've Just Read a Piece of the Greatest Library Ever Rebuilt

Thank you for reading.

This book is one of thousands we're restoring, reimagining, and translating as part of the **Modern Library of Alexandria** — a global movement to preserve and share humanity's most important ideas.

What was once lost to fire and time is now rising again — not just as memory, but as living, breathing knowledge, freely accessible to all.

What You Can Do Next:

- **Keep Reading.**

  Discover more legendary works — in beautiful print, audiobook, or digital form — at LibraryofAlexandria.com.

- **Build Your Own Library.**

  Every title is available as a paperback, hardcover, or collectible boxset — at true printing cost. Craft a personal library worthy of display.

- **Spread the Light.**

  Share this book. Tell others about the movement. Help us translate every timeless work into every language, so no reader is ever left behind.

By finishing this book, you've already taken part in something extraordinary.

Join us at LibraryofAlexandria.com

Together, we're rebuilding the greatest library the world has ever known.

With appreciation,
The Modern Library of Alexandria Team

Visit:

www.libraryofalexandria.com

Or scan the code below: